Mozart to Metallica: Connections between Classical Music and Heavy Metal

By:

Michael See

ISBN

Dedication

This book is dedicated to:

My family – for putting up with my music.

Mrs. Elliot – for teaching me how to be a musician.

KC – for all the concerts, and more to come.

Table of Contents

1
Intro

I'm just a guy, a Dad, a teacher, a musician, a metalhead!

My musical journey began long before I was a metalhead. Long before I was a musician. My musical journey started with my mom's record collection, yes, the old 33LPs. There is something to be said about the influence of music during a person's teenage years and my mom graduated high school in 1961. As teenagers, we start to move away from the musical tastes of our parents and start to enjoy and experience other styles of music. These new styles of music will then have an impact on us throughout our entire lives. My mom's teenage years were in the late 1950s and early '60s. This was the time when early rock and roll was emerging. Her record collection consisted of Oldies (a very loose term these days), even early oldies. Bill Haley and the Comets - Rock Around the Clock, Chuck Berry - My Maybelline, The Big Bopper - Chantilly Lace, Jerry Lee Lewis - Great Balls of Fire, and Elvis. Even more modern albums of Neil Diamond - The Jazz Singer, Kenny Rogers - The Gambler, and a whole lot more. I was always drawn to the great guitar gods that were Chuck Berry and Dick Del. Later during high school, I became a big Beatles fan. My mom remembers going to see the Beatles movie, *Help!* When it came out in theaters, she never did see *Hard Day's Night or Yellow Submarine.* Mom was always more of an Elvis fan than a Beatles fan.

My first connection to metal was my older half-brother when he came to live with us for a few years. He was a rebellious teenager, and I was 8. He was (and still is) a big Ozzy Osbourne fan. I believe it was a Blizzard of Ozz poster on his wall that my parents HATED. We were a pretty conservative household, and that music was not played. I remember hearing my parents talking about KISS and how it might(??) stand for *Knights in Service to Satan*. But they still allowed my brother to paint his face like Gene Simmons for Halloween. Mom even helped. I didn't get to listen to much of the music from Ozzy during that time, but I remember the reactions of my parents towards it. It always made me wonder, "What makes it so bad?"

When I was in 6th grade, I went to the next step on my musical journey and began playing trumpet. I will forever be grateful to Mrs. Elliott for being my first band teacher and somehow surviving us, as little kids learning to play instruments from nothing to making some basic version of music at our first concert. *God Bless all first-year band teachers. There will be a special place in Heaven for you!*

I continued playing trumpet though middle school and high school, where I also started playing baritone (think small tuba…). High school band became my go-to place to hang out. Band became my friend group. It's where I met the lady that would eventually become my wife. I still talk to band friends from high school. I continued playing both instruments into college, where I learned a higher level of appreciation for the music. I was playing trumpet for marching band, jazz band, pep band, and playing baritone for wind ensembles. Playing and being exposed to more and more traditional music in the Wind Ensemble.

Playing music gives a person a different experience of music versus simply listening to it. For example, ask my wife to play a Sousa march and she'll get angry. She is determined that John Philip Sousa had an ex-girlfriend who played French horn, so he wrote bad French horn parts. (I have no idea if that is true or not…) The french horn parts for most Sousa marches are just off beat notes through most of the song, over, and over and over…. Ask any French horn player. I learned the classic rock song *Breadfan* by Budgie (which originally came out in 1973) because it was the opening song for our marching band show during my junior year of high school. It was a very quick pace and the first move, the entire trumpet line had to play the opening riff while trying not to trip over the drumline. Metallica then put it on their 1998 Garage Inc album. Every time I hear the Metallica cover, my brain goes back to that opening move of the marching show.

There were two key points when I started becoming a metal head. The first was my 18th birthday when I received the newly released Led Zeppelin *BBC Sessions* album. This gift changed my world, as it does for many high schoolers who first discovered one of the greatest bands ever. Again, the influence of music during your teenage years. The second key point was when I first went off to tech school. One of my roommates kept playing this one particular album and the more I listened to it, the more I liked it: Metallica's *Black* album. That was it. I was hooked on metal. Within a few months, I owned Black album, Reload, Garage, Inc, Ride the Lightning, and just kept adding more. I even got to see (not hear) Megadeth in person when they were doing a promotional signing event at a local store promoting their *Cryptic Writings* album in 1999. I didn't even really know who they were, other than I had heard the name Megadeth. I would later learn the connection between them and my (now) favorite band, Metallica.

And then there were concerts. It started with seeing Santana (1999) while I was living in Phoenix (again, the really good guitar playing), Creed - with Sevendust and Nickelback opening (2000), and then…Ozzfest 2001!!

Ozzfest was nearly a religious experience. I believe it was 32,000 fans that packed The Gorge Amphitheater in Washington. This is my first big Metal experience. This went beyond "just going to a concert." This was a festival atmosphere. Three stages. Beer Garden. Tattoo shop. All the merch stands. All the metal shirts. The leather. The hair. I was blown away. I walked past a couple walking around with a baby (less than 3 months old) wearing a onesie from one of the bands. I watched people getting updated tattoos to add to the list of Ozzfests they had attended. Of course, the line for the porta-potties was horrible. At one point, I had to ditch my friends to go find water. Drowning Pool was the first band we saw. They wanted the crowd to jump when *Let the Bodies Hit the Floor* dropped...but the single had not yet hit the West Coast so no one in the crowd knew the song. No one knew what to do. The second time through the chorus, we figured it out.

The lineup for Ozzfest included (in reverse order of appearance) Black Sabbath, Marilyn Manson, Papa Roach, Linkin Park, Crazy Town (they were big…for a bit), Zakk Wylde, and Disturbed!! Disturbed got moved up from the 2nd stage to be the opener on the main stage. There were some other bands like Taproot, American Head Charge, Godhead, and so many others. One of the biggest moments of the day, for me, was when Black Sabbath started into *War Pigs*. 32,000 people who all knew the words, screaming in unison the opening lines. At that point in time, I didn't know the story of Black Sabbath, I didn't know their full impact on music, but I knew how that moment made me feel…and I was hooked.

So many more concerts followed (at the time of writing) Metallica (3x), Iron Maiden (3x), Dream Theater (2x), Flogging Molly, Motley Crue (2x), Tool (2x), Trans-Siberian Orchestra (x3), Coheed and Cambria, Mastodon, Volbeat, Halestorm, and so many others.

Why write this book?

The original idea for this book came while I was going to college. Being a musician but not a music major, most of my elective courses were music classes. One of my favorites was *Master Works of Music* taught by Dr. Ilse Marie-Lee (now retired) at Montana State University. The outline of the course was pretty simple - we would explore 8 classic master works of music, learn about the composers, and why those pieces have a special place in the world of music. This also happened to be the time I really was getting to learn the backstory and history of metal music. *That Metal Show* was airing on VH1 Classic. I would watch it every chance I got. I loved hearing stories directly from the artists. In class I was learning about Classical music and on TV I was learning about Metal music.

The more I listened to both styles: Metal and Classical, the more connections I started seeing. I actually started to collect my thoughts as a fake term paper. Not for any class but with the same format, because I didn't know any other format to write in. I just started writing. I remember it started as three pages, and then I realized I didn't know as much as I thought. I kept the document on a hard drive for years thinking that I would add to it, but eventually gave up on the idea. About 17 years after I wrote the first three pages, the idea kept nagging at me. I was watching several YouTube channels that were reaction videos. "*Classical Composer reacts to *name of metal song**." I was relearning the basics of music that I had played years before and how it applied to metal music. As I watched these videos, I kept thinking back to the original paper I wrote. I would think through different parts and connections and keep thinking back to the original idea. One day, I just started typing. It began with all the random thoughts and an outline, what eventually came out is what you are reading. In the 17 years, I have learned more stories, read so many books, and listened to hours and hours of head-banging music.

This book is written for the metalheads. Anyone who has been told that metal music isn't real music. "It's too loud." "It sucks." "Pop music is better." Metalheads are a loyal fan base because we must be. We must stick up for our music every time. Metal is often written off because it rubs people the wrong way, because of the imagery, the perceived Satanic overtones, and a thousand other reasons.

The worlds of heavy metal music and classical music are often not discussed together. They are seen as distant cousins. If there was a Venn diagram showing the overlapping sections of the two genres of music, many people would never think to put them on the same page. The imagery of classical music evokes tuxedos, champagne flowing, a night on the town, those funny little opera glasses. Sophistication. Heavy metal makes people think of long hair, leather jackets, silver studs, black concert t-shirts. General loudness.

This book hopes to show the ways the two forms of music overlap and intertwine with each other because of the use of storytelling, connections to politics, trying to create more sound, embracing different key signatures and time signatures, connections with the occult, having extremely talented musicians, and delving deep into dark subjects. Heavy Metal and Classical have more connections than most people realize.

This book is written for classical musicians. The nerd musician who wants to learn more about different types of music. The person that grew up playing music that fits into a certain box but knows there's more music out there. Other music that is fun to play. More music that is as much of a challenge to play as anything.

My hope is for both sides and anyone else, to have a deeper and better understanding of both types of music. You don't have to like it all, but maybe you will appreciate it more. There are so many more examples of the different topics I could have put in but didn't. Maybe you will go out and try to find more.

Interactive

This book is intended to be interactive. In addition to the text, I have created a playlist so that you, as the reader, can hear the amazing music that is discussed in the book and learn more about it. Enjoy!

To access, install and open Spotify on your connected device, go to Search and find the camera option. Scan the code below. I will also include this code at the beginning of each chapter. Due to legal reasons and Spotify rules, I could not create codes for individual songs, so I had to create the whole playlist. Enjoy the unique playlist that puts Pantera next to Chopin!

2.
A Good Story

Music should have a purpose. Music should have a story. A reason. Something to tell. Something more than being "Hot in the club" or "Shakin' that ass." Not that we don't all need a good ass shaking once in a while. (Have you seen that video from Mastodon?) "Girl, baby baby" just doesn't get me excited or pull me into the music. Just like any good book, music is better with a plot line, characters, protagonists, antagonists, drama, and all those other fun words you learned in high school English class. I know I will receive some hate for this, but my favorite song that has a great story is a country song. (Gasp!!) *The Gambler* by Kenny Rogers provides an excellent example of how to put a good story in music. It has characters, plot, and climax. Not only did the song push Kenny Rogers into mass stardom, it also spawned a 5-movie series starring Kenny himself. The story is written from the perspective of a young man onboard a train that is sharing the space with an old man that has seen some miles in his life. The old man asks for a drink of the young man's whiskey and proceeds to give him advice about life.

A large portion of what most people would consider "Classical music" was not just written to be played but written to be entertainment. In the modern era, we have movies with incredible soundtracks. We get the visual story with the music supporting it. Classical musicians wrote operas as entertainment. Instead of going to a movie theater, they went to an opera. Operas have all of those entertaining English words with heroes and drama and comedy, and the music was not just supporting the plot but was a part of the production. The actors were trained singers who would belt out the libretto, or the words of the music, not just speaking lines from a script.

Let's jump into some examples. One of my favorite pieces of music is the climax to Mozart's opera *Don Giovanni.*

Don Giovanni - Wolfgang Amadeus Mozart

Mozart's outrageous comedy tells the tale of an incorrigible young playboy who blazes a path to his own destruction in a single day. Based on the story of Don Juan, *Don Giovanni* follows an irresistible (yet irresponsible and amoral) youth who is loved by women almost as universally as he loves them. It doesn't take long before the audience sees that even Don Giovanni cannot escape the consequences of his flouting of conventional morality.

And in the climax of the story, a statue of *Il Commendatore*, who is the father of the young woman that Don Giovanni is trying to seduce, comes to life and tells Don Giovanni to change his lustful ways or die.

Act 1 - We see a masked Don Giovanni rushing out of a house and being pursued by Donna Anna. The excitement awakens her father, the Commendatore, and a duel ensues. Don Giovanni kills the Commendatore, and Donna Anna's fiancé Ottavio. (*yes, she was engaged and having relations with Don Giovanni!!*) Ottavio vows to avenge the Commendatore's death.

The next day, Don Giovanni and his servant, Leporello, run into Donna Elvira, who is seeking the man who betrayed her. Of course, it was Don Giovanni, but he was in a mask, so she did not recognize him. He tries to console her but is forced to flee when she realizes who he is. Leporello is left to tell Donna Elvira that she is just the next girl in a long line of women.

Leporello joins Don Giovanni at a wedding, where he is flirting with Zerlina. Anna and Ottavio arrive at the wedding, asking everyone for assistance to find her father's killer. Because of the mask, she does not recognize Don Giovanni. Elvira appears to warn everyone about Don Giovanni, but he makes another miraculous escape. Back at Don Giovanni's house, everyone is having a good time with the wedding guests. Anna, Ottavio, and Elvria appear in masks. Don Giovanni is in the other room with Zerlina. She screams. Everyone rushes to help. Don Giovanni makes another escape.

Photo Credit - Sarasota Opera

Act 2 - Don Giovanni and Leporello trade clothes so Don Giovanni can try to woo Elvira's maid. An angry mob appears and mistakes Leporello for Don Giovanni. Don Giovanni (still dressed as Leporello) even offers to help the mob, but not before convincing them to give him the weapons. Don Giovanni makes another escape. Leporello exposes his identity, and the mob goes hunting again. Leporello joins his master in the cemetery, and they hear a voice from the statue of The Commendatore. It is a warning of impending doom. Don Giovanni thinks it is a joke and even invites the statue to a banquet. At the banquet, Elvira begs Don Giovanni to change his life and marry her, but he refuses. The statue appears again to tell Don Giovanni to repent of his ways. He refuses and he is sent to the fiery depths of hell.

Not only is Don Giovanni an exciting and powerful opera, it introduces themes that can connect to modern ideas. *Do you know any players that sleep around too much? Do they get hunted down by dads or boyfriends?* There are many opera examples that can show great story lines, and we will get to those, but metal music can, and often does, follow the same idea of a plot line, characters, protagonists, etc.

Don Giovanni is the story of a playboy who somehow escapes getting caught multiple times over a couple of days. Sword fights. Jumping off balconies. He even uses his servant as a scapegoat to distract a mob. Eventually, his actions caught up to him in the form of a ghost of the man he killed. Don Giovanni refuses to change his lustrous ways and seals his fate as he falls into hell. That is a fun and exciting story. That story could be developed into a larger plot line with several more daring escapes and a big fiery Michael Bay-style ending. This style of opera is common with good story lines, exciting characters, and dramatic endings. The downside of opera, at least for many Americans, is that they are performed in a different language. Usually Italian, German, or sometimes Spanish. Unless you speak that language, it can be difficult to connect to the music.

To make an easier connection, let's look at an example of a good example of a great story, and it's in English. The two stories share themes of rebellion, individualism, and some supernatural elements.

2112 - Rush

Influenced by the writings of Ayn Rand. Based in the future, in the year 2112, a galaxy-wide war results in the union of all planets under the rule of the Red Star of the Solar Federation. The world is controlled by the "Priests of the Temples of Syrinx," who determine the content of all reading matter, songs, pictures – every facet of life.

Section 1 - Overture

In classical music, the overture is a short combination of all the songs of a long piece of music played before the curtain goes up. In 2112, it is a similar story. In this opening instrumental section, we hear themes from the upcoming sections. No vocals are heard except at the end, at a near whisper.

Section 2 - Temples of Syrinx

In the 2nd section, we are introduced to the city of Megadon and the Priests of the Temple of Syrinx who make an announcement telling the people they are in charge. They control every aspect of life from the art to entertainment and that everyone needs to join their way of life.

Section 3 - Discovery

In part 3, we are introduced to the protagonist, someone who lives in this controlled world. He makes a musical discovery (a guitar?) and begins to play. He has never heard anything like it as music has been banned from their world. He finds a new joy in life and wants to share his newfound happiness.

Section 4 - Presentation

In part 4, the protagonist takes the instrument to Megadon city to present it before the Priests. They immediately reject the idea as it is outside of their way of life. They then smash the guitar into pieces, leaving our hero distraught and rejected.

Section 5 - Oracle: The Dream

Devastated, the main character wanders the streets and falls asleep. He is met by an Oracle. The Oracle shows him a vision of the past, where music and art were a part of the culture.

Section 6 - Soliloquy

In part 6, our hero wakes up in a cave, where he has stayed for many days. He realizes that he cannot live in this highly controlled world, but he has nowhere else to go. He falls into a deep depression.

Big Guitar solo…Instrumental…

Section 7 - The Grand Finale

Instrumental climax! Boom! Crash! The planet is taken over by the Solar Federation.

The 20-minute epic journey that Rush takes us on gives us themes of government control and new awakenings, visions of the past, and lamenting of the present. Why things are bad. Finding new things.

Love, romance, courtship, and other similar topics have always worked as inspiration for composers. These topics evoke big emotions. It makes it easier for an audience to connect to. We have all had similar things happen in our lives. Love is the central theme to the next example; it takes the entire opera to find out.

Turandot - Puccini

A familiar storyline that even shows up in Disney movies like Brave or Aladdin, where suitors are competing to win the heart of the princess. The original story was written in Italian by Giuseppe Adami and Renato Simoni, then the music was written for the opera by Giacomo Puccini in 1926.

(Is it pronounced Tur-An-DOT or Tur-An-DOUGH? Depends on who you ask...even Puccini and the writers couldn't agree.)

The story - Any prince seeking to marry Princess Turandot must answer three riddles. If he fails, he will die.

Act 1 - The story takes place in a mythical version of Peking, China. It opens on a crowd watching an execution. It has been decreed that anyone that wishes to be a suitor to the princess, Turanadot, must successfully answer three riddles, or die trying…and this man, who is about to be executed, failed! Someone in the crowd, Calaf, recognizes the condemned man as his long-lost father. Princess Turandot appears, and our hero Calaf is overcome by the princess' beauty and announces that he will be the next suitor.

Photo Credit - The Metropolitan Opera

Act 2 - In the palace, everyone is trying to convince Calaf that he should back out of the challenge. The princess gives the three riddles and Calaf is successful in answering the questions. Turandot begs her father to not allow the marriage, but Calaf offers another solution. Can the princess guess his name?

Act 3 - No one in the kingdom is allowed to sleep until the Princess learns the stranger's name. Calaf's friends are tortured to give up the answer. Calaf's friend resists the torture, and Turandot is impressed. Liu says it is love that makes her strong, and she grabs a knife and kills herself. Turandot feels emotion for the first time and announces that the stranger's name is Love.

Turandot is a love story at heart that also gives us one of the greatest and most well-known opera songs ever written - Nessun Dorma. *Nessun Dorma* translates to "none shall sleep." It is a victorious song sung from the perspective of Calaf. The very loud climax of Nessun Dorma is Calaf professing, "I will win Turandot's hand in marriage." The passage has turned into a victory cry for other purposes. In 1990, Italy used the 1972 recording of tenor Luciano Pavarotti to promote the World Cup. Many Italians now use the song as a hype song of "I will win!"

The 1991 performance of Nessun Dorma by the Three Tenors - Plácido Domingo, José Carreras, and Luciano Pavarotti, on the eve of the World Cup became an instant hit, the three won a Grammy for Best Classical Vocal Performance and the album went on to be the best-selling classical album of all time.

Other big emotions can also inspire good music. Fear can be a good muse. Being in an unforgettable situation and fearing for one's life is the subject of the next example.

The Count of Tuscany - Dream Theater

The Count of Tuscany appears on the 2009 album *Black Clouds and Silver Linings* by Dream Theater. The song is written by guitarist John Petrucci about an adventure he went on with his guitar tech on a visit to the Italian countryside.

Our storyteller travels to a foreign land and meets The Count of Tuscany. The Count takes him on a journey to a large estate out in the country. The Count introduces his brother, an older gentleman. The storyteller feels afraid and unsure. The brother shows him around the estate, including down into the wine cellars, where they would hide soldiers during the war. But the soldiers never left. They died in the cellars as prisoners. The storyteller is afraid he may never leave the house. The Count sees his guests' fear and explains that the whole thing is a prank they like to play on tourists. They promise this grand adventure and then try to scare them.

The lyrics are anecdotal, recalling an event that took place during the band's *Train of Thought* tour whereby Petrucci and his guitar technician were taken to visit an Italian Count's mansion. This story was then confirmed by the winery itself, *Villa Calcinaia* near Florence, Italy. Niccolo Capponi recalls meeting these two "rock and roll" guys who didn't fit the mold. They were "square, family men who were very musically cultured." He remembers taking the pair around the vineyards and the property, smoking his pipe, as usual. He does not recall intentionally trying to scare anyone.

While the perceived fear certainly created a good story, according to the actual host, his visitors were in no real danger. Maybe they were in danger, maybe they weren't. Either way, it made a great song. Our next story is a lesser-known opera, but the storyline has so many twists and turns you might need a chart to follow along.

La Forza Del Destino - Verdi

Written in 1909, Guiseppi Verdi's tale of ill-fated love, revenge, and family strife is a modern tale. The Story - Lenora is the daughter of the General and Alvaro is the poor young love interest. The couple tries to elope, but Lenora's father is accidentally killed in a struggle, sparking a series of events including the country going to war. Carlo, Lernora's brother, seeks revenge for their father's murder. Lernora flees the city and devotes herself to God at the nearby monastery.

Alvaro is drafted into the army and must go to war. Alvaro ends up saving Carlos' life, not knowing who each other are. They become friends. Carlos eventually discovers Alvaro's true identity, they have a fight, and Alvaro cuts his own face in order to not kill Carlos. He, too, vows to enter a monastery. After five years, Carlos finds Alvaro. Lernoa appears, and everyone recognizes each other, Carlos takes a mortal wound, but not before mortally wounding Lenora. As she dies, she tells Alvaro that she will wait for him in heaven.

La Forza is a long story that takes place over 5 years. It has a love story, death, military, and war. It creates a lifelong story about how people change. The next example covers three different songs written by the same group but is a continuation of the same story as they grow up and learn about life.

Unforgiven I, II, II - Metallica

The trio of songs from the band Metallica layout a lifetime of pain, regret, and life lessons. Part 1 of the trilogy appears on the 1991 Black album. Part 2 on 1997's ReLoad. And the final installment of 2008's Death Magnetic. With 17 years between the beginning and the end, audiences were left with parts of an uncompleted story, and yet each section is a standalone lesson on life.

Part 1 - Being born into a life where people let him down.

Part 2 - Trying to find love and trusting people

Part 3 - Having regrets and accepting the blame for yourself

There is a fantastic breakdown of the trilogy that I wish I could take credit for, but there is not an author's name on the blog - https://amritkosaraju.blogspot.com/

The Unforgiven

In "The Unforgiven", the singer speaks about growing up in a strict and uptight society. He grows up doing as he's told and not thinking or living for himself. The young man is not afforded the chance to make his own decisions. Other people (parents, relatives, etc.?) live his life for him. The young man tries to live up to their expectations and does his best to be the person they want him to be.

Though he wants to be the man others expect him to be, the young man is constantly battling (with himself), as his heart and interests lie elsewhere. He can't win this fight, as one way or another, he loses.

The young man becomes "old", but not literally. He is tired, and becomes like an old man, and he no longer cares, he has given up on life. He realizes that he has done nothing with his life and is filled with regret.

He becomes tired and bitter and starts to blame those people who controlled and lived his life. The young man becomes resentful of these people for not letting him live life his own way and cannot ever forgive them for this.

The Unforgiven II

This song picks up a few years after from where "The Unforgiven" leaves us. The young man is now an adult. He has left behind all the people who controlled him and has found someone he cares for. He might be falling for this person, but he still has doubts. The door here is a metaphor. A door to his own heart. Should he open it yet?

This person he has fallen/ about to fall for has also been through the same things as the "young man". The young man still doesn't trust this other person completely. The "young man" is asking the person if they can be there for him. He is prepared to be there for her, but is she? Or is she just like those "unforgiven" people, who tried to control him and his life. The "young man" then asks himself if she loves him. He is probably plucking the petals of a flower, searching for an answer. He concludes that she indeed does love him and that she will stay with him.

He decides to give her a chance and starts to trust her and love her. The sun brings in light, which is a metaphor for hope. The "young man" believes that he has found someone like himself and hopes to spend his time with her. He takes the key to his heart and buries it in her. Here by unforgiven, he means that she is an outcast, an unforgiven to the other people, just like he is.

The Unforgiven III

The singer here speaks of a person, who might have damaged his life. He also speaks constantly about "sailing" and traveling in a ship and of seas. I think this is a metaphor for the journey of life itself. He has got nowhere to go and is "lost in life" as one might say. But he argues. He tells us of how he searched for the good things in life, but has ended up cold and alone.

He finally comes to realize that he has nobody to blame – not the ones who controlled him as a "young man", not the person he loved as an adult – but himself. It is his fault that he hasn't done anything with his life. It is his fault that he has ended up alone. The young man seeks forgiveness. But it is revealed that he is indeed asking forgiveness from himself. In fact, he blames himself and wants to be forgiven for not living a better life.

In the end, he is still left regretting his life. But he comes to an understanding that he has to blame himself. He brands himself as "the unforgiven". He asks forgiveness from himself for having failed in life.

Metallica's Unforgiven trilogy shows the growth of a person throughout their life, learning to love, and accepting who he is. Similar to *Unforgiven*, the next story shows how decisions may not have the outcomes that you hope, and sometimes they can have tragic endings. The two stories share themes of personal desires being outweighed by societal norms, consequences of actions, and personal transformation.

Tannhauser - Wagner

"This opera begins in an orgy and ends in the heavens, with a fascinating contrast between the sacred and profane, the damnation and the salvation, the flesh and the soul."

Premiering in 1861, Tannhauser is considered one of Wagner's easier operas to digest. The opera touches on subjects of love, lust, friendship, morals, death and salvation. This opera is one of several of Wagner's pieces that are considered '*Gesamtkunstwerk*' or the totality of the work of art. Wagner was not only the composer of the music, but he was also the *librettist*, or the one who wrote the words for the story.

The story is based on a medieval myth. Wagner found the actual Wartburg Castle. In the opera, Elisabeth is based on an actual person, Saint Elisabeth of Thuringia. She married at the age of 14 and lived in Castle Wartburg, then widowed at the age of 20. She used her money to build a hospital and used it for charity. She died at the age of 24 and was later sainted.

Act 1

In the early 13th century, in Thüringen, Germany, Tannhauser who is a knight and minstrel spends time with Venus who is the Goddess of lust. But Tannhauser is tired of life with Venus. He leaves the forbidden place, Venusberg.

Tannhauser goes back to reality, which is a place near the castle of Wartburg. Some friends of Tannhauser asked him where he had been until then. Tannhauser refuses to answer their questions, and he attempts to leave. Then, one of his friends, Wolfram, reminds him that Elisabeth, who was Tannhauser's lover, has been waiting for him for a long time.

Act 2

In Wartburg castle, Landgrave Hermann holds a song contest and declares that the winner will be awarded the prize by his daughter,

Elisabeth. Among a lot of nobles and knights, Hermann gives challengers the subject of their song. It is "Essence of Love." Wolfram sings that the Essence of Love is Platonic. But Tannhauser sings that it is the pleasures of lust, and he praises Venus. The audience knows that Tannhauser visited Venus in the forbidden place, Venusberg. All people insist he be banished. However, Elisabeth appeals to them to stop. She asserts that she is the most deeply hurt. Landgrave Hermann orders Tannhauser to visit the Pope in order to pay for what he has done.

Act 3

Several months later, Elisabeth doesn't find Tannhauser among pilgrims from Rome. So, she decides to go to heaven. Then, Tannhauser comes back from Rome, and he tells his friend, Wolfram, that Tannhauser's penitence was refused. Tannhauser attempts to visit Venus again. Wolfram stops him. Then, the coffin, in which Elisabeth is laid, is carried past them. Tannhauser takes his last breath, because he is shocked to see her. But his soul is saved. Elisabeth's death brings about his salvation.

Tannhauser is finally saved but finds out too late. His love is gone. The decisions he made earlier came back to haunt him with tragic endings. The next story originated from Ireland and is about an outlaw who is betrayed by the woman he loves.

Whiskey in the Jar

This song was not only popularized on Metallica's 1997 cover album *Garage, Inc.,* but that band was covering the 1973 version from the band Thin Lizzy, who in turn was covering The Dubliners very folksy 1967 version. Evidence that a great story can make a great song with so many groups wanting to cover the same tune. It was a popular live song by many other bands including The Grateful Dead, The Pogues, Burl Ives, Peter Paul and Mary, and U2 to name a few.

All these versions were based on the same story that came out of Ireland around 1650, during the time of Oliver Cromwell. The origins of the story are not as well-known as the tune itself, but it is based on an actual person, *Patrick Fleming*. Fleming was a criminal and outlaw. His exploits are documented in several other poems from the era.

The story is about a *Highwayman* (or robber - Fleming) who robs an Englishman while they are traveling. Fleming would usually only engage with English nobility or higher-ranking military personnel (Cpt. Ferrel). After the robbery, he flees to the arms of his lover, Molly. The legend says Molly then betrays Fleming by jamming his gun. When Captain Ferrel shows up, Fleming tries to shoot him, but his gun misfires. Fleming is then arrested and thrown in jail.

The Metallica version of a simple robbery is a much nicer version than that of the real Patrick Fleming story. The other poems and stories of Fleming paint a picture of a much viler and more inhumane criminal. He was eventually caught, but only because of Molly's betrayal, then later, executed for his crimes.

Excerpt from

The Ballad of Patrick Fleming

Written in 1684

Patrick Flemming was a Vallient Soldier,
He carried his Blunderbuss upon his shouldier
He cockt his Pistol and drew his Rapier,
Stand and deliver for I am the taker fal, lal,

If you're Patrick Flemming as I do suppose you be,
We are three Pedlars a ganging so free sir,
We are three Pedlars a ganging to Dublin,
Nothing at all in ur Pockets but our loading.

Says Patrick Flemming prithe don't trifle,
For I am resolved Your packs for to rifle,
Here is a bank on which they must rest on,
To search tham all I have a Commission.

Loath they were to do as he commanded,
But knowing Patrick charg's double-handed,
Searching their packs most carefully round,
There did he find four Hundred pound.

Oh! I have two brothers they're both in the army
The one is at Cork and the other at Kilkenny,
If they were here both blyth and bonny,
I'd rather see them than any one dear honey.

As I was going over Ruberry mountain,
Gold and silver there was counting
He thought it little I thought it better,
I took the Gold from Colonel Pepper.

My Whore she proved false and that is the reason
Or else Patrick Flemming had never been taken,
When I was asleep and knew nothing of the matter
Then she loaded my arms with Water:

Oh Patrick Flemming how often have I told you
With Swords with Pistols we would surround You,
For kissing of other mens wives brisk and merry,
as You was going to Londonderry.

Author's Note - I wish Metallica would have taken the opportunity to create an epic movie-style music video with a period accurate tale of the story from Whiskey in the Jar. I think it would have been a fun way to tell the story in a more literal way. It would give the audience a chance to learn some history about the original folktale. Instead, they opted for a basic house party with the band playing in the living room and the party guests trashing the house.

The old folktale of the criminal Patrick Flemming is retold by several bands, usually in a calmer, less violent version of the story. The original story has been nearly forgotten. A similar theme continues in the next story. A real-life example where the details have been lost through retelling of the story many times.

The Trooper/Charge of the Light Brigade

So many connections here. The same story that comes from real-life, shared through music and poetry. Someone even made a movie about it.

The Iron Maiden song *The Trooper* was on the 1983 album *Piece of Mind*, which was written by bass player Steve Harris....

...that was based on the song *The Charge of the Light Brigade* written as an instrumental piece by Max Steiner in 1875...

...that was based on the Alfred Lord Tennyson poem *Charge of the Light Brigade*, written the same year as the actual event in 1854.

Oct 25, 1854 - 600 men rode into battle, led by Lord Cardigan (yes, the sweater of this style was named after this guy), as part of the Crimean War. The order to charge into battle proved disastrous as the order was riddled with miscommunication and misinformation. The command to attack was started by Lord Raglan with the understanding that the Light and Heavy Brigades (horseback soldiers) would attack with a large force of infantry to follow behind.

There was a miscommunication, and the infantry was severely delayed. The two commanders of the brigades decided to follow the ill-interpreted orders and led the 670 horse-carried men, sabers drawn, into a more-than-mile-long front, with Russian forces firing on 3 sides. Witnesses told of the horror that ensued. Blood-spattered bodies, missing limbs, and heads exploded, which all erupted into a mass casualty event. In all, 110 men were dead, and another 160 were wounded. In addition to the large loss of manpower, over 400 hundred horses were lost. Considered one of the greatest failures in military history and a great lesson in the importance of communication on the battlefield.

Photo Credit - ultimate-guitar.com -

Iron Maiden's mascot, Eddie, dressed as The Trooper

Charge of the Light Brigade

By Alfred Lord Tennyson

I

Half a league, half a league,

Half a league onward,

All in the valley of Death

Rode the six hundred.

"Forward, the Light Brigade!

Charge for the guns!" he said.

Into the valley of Death

Rode the six hundred.

II

"Forward, the Light Brigade!"

Was there a man dismayed?

Not though the soldier knew

Someone had blundered.

Theirs not to make reply,

Theirs not to reason why,

Theirs but to do and die.

Into the valley of Death

Rode the six hundred.

III

Cannon to right of them,

Cannon to left of them,

Cannon in front of them

Volleyed and thundered;

Stormed at with shot and shell,

Boldly they rode and well,

Into the jaws of Death,

Into the mouth of hell

Rode the six hundred.

IV

Flashed all their sabres bare,

Flashed as they turned in air

Sabring the gunners there,

Charging an army, while

All the world wondered.

Plunged in the battery-smoke

Right through the line they broke;

Cossack and Russian

Reeled from the sabre stroke

Shattered and sundered.

Then they rode back, but not

Not the six hundred.

V

Cannon to right of them,

Cannon to left of them,

Cannon behind them

Volleyed and thundered;

Stormed at with shot and shell,

While horse and hero fell.

They that had fought so well

Came through the jaws of Death,

Back from the mouth of hell,

All that was left of them,

Left of six hundred.

VI

When can their glory fade?

O the wild charge they made!

All the world wondered.

Honour the charge they made!

Honour the Light Brigade,

Noble six hundred!

While the Tennyson version is written in the third person, telling the story as someone watching the event, the Iron Maiden version is written from first-person perspective, as if you were on the battlefield. The song talks about the fervor of the soldiers' mentality during the battle and their willingness to kill the opponent. It describes the sweat from the horses and the smell of gunpowder from the canons. The story ends as the bodies begin to pile up and the soldier gets shot by a Russian and draws his last breath.

While we are on the topic of writing songs about real-life events, Iron Maiden has more. The band does like to take good stories from all around the world and turn them into amazing songs.

Run to the Hills - Iron Maiden

Run to the Hills is about the European explorers arriving in the "New World," the America continent. The song came out on the seminal Iron Maiden album *Number of the Beast* in 1982.

Songwriter Steve Harris wanted the song to literally feel like galloping horses as the natives are fleeing. The galloping can be heard in the percussion beat. The song is written from three different perspectives.

Part 1 - Written from the perspective of the native. The natives tell about the white man coming across the ocean, bringing disease, killing everything in their path, and becoming enslaved by the white man.

Part 2 - From the perspective of the white man. This account tells of chasing the "redman" around the desolate plains and killing them for the white man's gain.

Part 3 - From an impartial third-party, giving more facts than opinions. This section reads more like a headline from a newspaper about what is happening in the New World.

The band Anthrax also tackled this same theme on their 1987 song "*Indians*." This song discusses racism, apathy, hopelessness, and respect.

Wind of Change - Scorpions

Written about the fall of the Berlin Wall and the fall of Communism, or at least that's what many people believe. The German band Scorpions song *Wind of Change* was actually written about life in the Soviet Union, before the fall of Communism. In 1989, the Scorpions were invited to participate in the Moscow Music Peace Festival, which took place over two days and was very *Woodstock-like* in its nature, except with hard rock and heavy metal bands including Ozzy Osbourne and Mötley Crüe. This event was the first time that any hard rock acts were permitted to perform in soviet Russia. It was this event that prompted vocalist Klaus Meine to pen the lyrics to *Wind of Change*. Meine, along with the rest of the band, grew up in Hannover, West Germany, just 200 miles west of Berlin. There were clearly some similarities between growing up in the shadow of the Berlin Wall and seeing Soviet Russia.

It was just three months later that the Berlin Wall fell, and the song was recorded soon thereafter. Most people (including this author) associate the song with the fall of the Berlin Wall because of the music video that accompanied the release of the song. The video featured clips of the Berlin Wall being destroyed. The song became so popular that the band was asked to perform it for former Russian leader Mikhail Gorbachev at his 80th birthday celebration at London's Royal Albert Hall.

Other Stories

There is a large list of great songs that could have been researched for this book. Below is a list of a few more songs that take real-life events and put them into music.

The Clansman - Iron Maiden - Based on Scottish lore.

Aida - Verdi - An Ethiopian princess is enslaved in ancient Egypt.

One - Metallica - World War I serviceman is trapped in his own head after being injured in battle.

Phantom of the Opera - Iron Maiden, written before the Andrew Lloyd Weber version

The Ripper - Judas Priest - Jack the Ripper from England

44 Minutes - Megadeth - North Hollywood Shootout in 1997

Gettysburg - Iced Earth - American Civil War

Manhattan Project - Rush - The creation of the Atomic Bomb

Angel of Death - Slayer - Terrors that took place in the Nazi concentration camps

Read a Book, Write a Song

Artists take inspiration from everywhere. Nature, love, heartbreak, grief, history, and many different places. If a musician wants to incorporate a good story into their music, why not start with a good story already. There have been many songs and pieces of music work that have been based on books. Here are a few.

J.R.R. Tolkien Works

J.R.R. Tolkien is known for writing the *Lord of the Rings* trilogy and *The Hobbit*. Now translated in over 50 languages and into major motion pictures, these books have captured audiences for over 70 years. *The Hobbit* was originally published in 1937 with huge success and a sequel was expected. After a few lesser-known pieces were published, readers finally received *The Fellowship of the Ring*, *The Two Towers*, and *Return of the King* in 1954 and 1955. Published after Tolkein's death in 1977, his son brought readers the basis for many parts of the whole world, *The Silmarillion*.

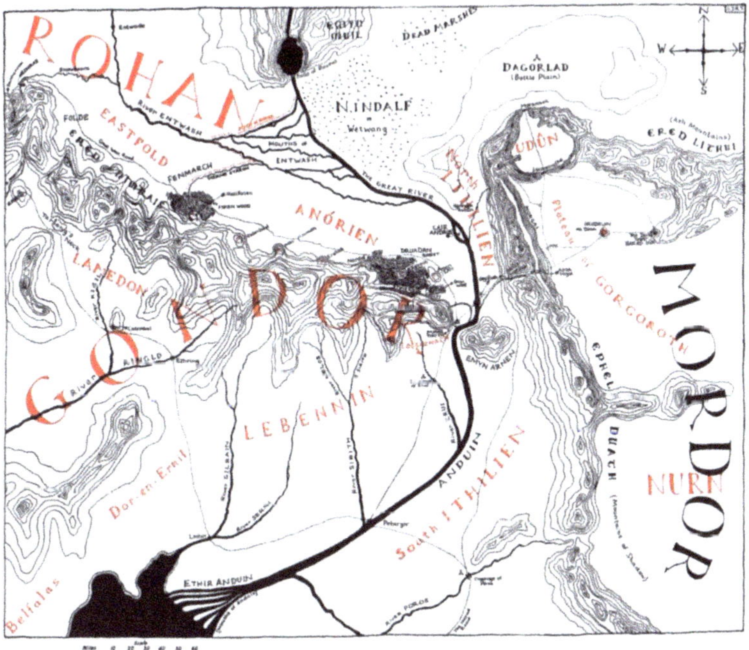

Original drawing done by Christopher Tolkien. Credit - tolkiengateway.net

Led Zeppelin gives us several songs that were based on Tolkien's works

- The Battle of Evermore (Led Zeppelin IV - 1970)
- Ramble On (Led Zeppelin II - 1969)

Lord of the Rings Suite

Not well known by most people, but a favorite among middle school and high school bands is the Symphony No. 1 The Lord of the Rings by Johan de Meji. Published in 1988, it takes inspiration directly from the original books. The movements include

- 1. Gandalf (The Wizard) includes a section about Shadowfax, Gandalf's horse.
- 2. Lothlorien (The Elvenwood)
- 3. Gollum (Sméagol)
- 4. Journey in the Dark
  - a. The Mines of Moria
  - b. The Bridge of Khazad-Dûm
- 5. Hobbits

Nightfall in Middle-Earth

The metal band Blind Guardian produced Nightfall in Middle-Earth in 1998. Based entirely on The Silmarillion. The band had done several individual songs based on Tolkien themes, but this was an entire album dedicated to the short tales talked about in The Silmarillion. Some of the tracks are not full songs but spoken narratives that further the story.

1. War of Wrath
2. Into the Storm
3. Lammoth
4. Nightfall
5. The Minstrel

6. The Curse of Fëanor
7. Captured
8. Blood Tears
9. Mirror Mirror
10. Face the Truth
11. Noldor (Dead Winter Reigns)
12. Battle of Sudden Flame
13. Time Stands Still (at the Iron Hill)
14. The Dark Elf
15. Thorn
16. The Eldar
17. Nom the Wise
18. When Sorrow Sang
19. Out on the Water
20. The Steadfast
21. A Dark Passage
22. Final Chapter (Thus Ends...)

Dune

Photo Credit - imdb.com

The science fiction novel *Dune* by Frank Herbert has now become a global phenomenon. Originally published in 1965, it is a favorite among sci-fi readers, not only for the original text, but also for the 5 related books that Herbert wrote and the many, many other books that his son has continued to add to the *Dune* universe.

During the 1970s, there was an attempt to turn the original book into a movie, including Salvador Dali as the Emperor, but it ultimately failed. Most people (*including myself*) were turned onto the world of *Dune* from the 1984 movie starring Kyle MacLachan. There was a mini-series done for television few people remember done in 2000. In 2019, the latest movie version came out with *Dune*, part 1 with part 2 premiering in 2024.

Iron Maiden decided to tackle the storyline on their 1983 album, *A Piece of Mind*. It has a great storyline, so Steve Harris decided to put it into music. Not only general themes, but there are names and terms taken directly from the story. The lyrics include terms from the book such as; Kwizatz Haderach, Gom Jabbar, and of course, the planet Dune. Iron Maiden asked Frank Herbert to use the name Dune as the title of the track, but he was apparently met with severe resistance, as he is adamantly opposed to heavy metal music. That is why the track title was changed to *To Tame a Land*.

Shakespeare

Felix Mendelssohn was only 17 when he wrote *A Midsummer Night's Dream*. Felix and his sister Fanny were raised as musicians. They were both well versed in instrumentation and composition, as well as multiple languages. When they were not writing or playing music, one of their favorite things to do was to read the works of Shakespeare. Written in 1843, sadly, near the end of his life, as Felix suffered multiple strokes in his early 20s, the piece invokes some of the fun and fantasy themes of the original play. The song captures visions of elves, fairies, and magical spells.

Poe

A Dream of Poe is a Doom Metal band originally from the Azores, Portugal. The duo incorporates themes and works of Edgar Allen Poe into all their music.

A few of their album titles

- Sorrow for the Lost Lenore (2009)
- Lady of Shalott (2010)
- The Mirror of Deliverance (2011)

Mythology

During all of my research, I started to notice that many of the songs I kept researching not only had a good story line but had similar topics and many of the songs were themed around Greek, Roman, and Norse mythology. So, I had to put them in a section all together.

Children of Zeus

Hercules

George Frideric Handel: The Choice of Hercules, HWV 69

Hercules was born a demi-god with incredible strength and stamina. Hercules defeated two snakes that were sent by his stepmother, Hera, while he was still a baby. Later in life, he had to complete 12 Labors to prove his worth; kill the Nemean Lion, kill the monster known as the Hydra who had nine venomous heads, capture the Cerynitian Hind, capture the Erymanthian Boar, Cleaning the Stables of Augeius in a day, drive away the Stymphalian Birds who were ravaging the countryside, bring back the Cretan Bull from Knossos, bring back the Mares of Diomedes, bring back Hippolyte's Girdle, bring back the cattle of Geryon, bring back the cattle of Geryon, and bring back Cerberus, the guard dog of the underworld.

Perseus

Carl Ditters von Dittersdorf: Symphony No. 4

Perseus is the hero who defeats Medusa. Medusa was a monster most known for having hair made of snakes and could turn anyone who looked upon her into stone. Perseus defeats her by using his mirrored shield and chops off her head.

The Minotaur and the Maze

The Cretan Labyrinth by Hieronymus Cock after Matthijs Cock, c.1558 © Ashmolean Museum

Shadowkeep - Minotaur

The Minotaur is a hulk of a monster with the head of a bull and the body of a human. The monster was imprisoned in a dark underground labyrinth at Knossos on the Aegean island of Crete. The Labyrinth was an ingenious maze commissioned by King Minos and designed by the architect Daedalus.

Iron Maiden - Flight of Icarus

To keep the secret of the maze, King Minos imprisoned Daedalus in the maze with his son Icarus. They were able to escape by creating wings made of feathers and wax. Icarus, however, ignored his father's warnings and flew too close to the sun. His wings melted, and he fell into the sea where he met his end.

Albert Roussel: Bacchus et Ariane, Op. 43, Suite No. 2

Photo of Bacchus et Ariane by Titan. Credit - https://www.nationalgallery.org.uk/

The story takes place after Thesus kills the Minotaur. Theusus rescues Ariane from the Minotaur and leaves her on the island of Naxos while she sleeps. Ariane wanders the beach looking for Theseus and is discovered by the God Baccus who falls in love with Ariane. He offers her the sky as a wedding present, seen in a constellation.

Achilles

Led Zeppelin - Achilles' Last Stand

Blind Guardian - And Then There Was Silence

The beginning of Achilles' story is mixed but he was the son of Peleus, a Greek king, and Thetis, a sea nymph or goddess. Achilles was mortal when he was born, unlike his mother. To make him immortal, his mother dips him in the river Styx or the mythical river that runs through the underworld. When Thetis held Achilles by the ankles to put him in the water, his ankles stayed dry and became his weakness.

Later, Achilles becomes the leader of the Troy army and goes on to defeat many armies. He is eventually killed because of an arrow to….his heel, of course, his one weak spot.

The Odyssey

The Odyssey - Symphony X
Odysseus - Max Bruch

The Odyssey is Homer's epic of Odysseus' 10-year struggle to return home after the Trojan War. While Odysseus battles mythical creatures and faces the wrath of the gods, his wife Penelope and his son Telemachus stave off suitors vying for Penelope's hand and Ithaca's throne long enough for Odysseus to return. The Odyssey ends as Odysseus wins a contest to prove his identity, slaughters the suitors, and retakes the throne of Ithaca.

Norse Mythology

Richard Wagner - Ride of the Valkyries

Amon Amarth - Twilight of the Thunder Gods, or really, most things about Viking culture

Manowar - Gods of War

Led Zeppelin - Immigrant Song

Norse mythology covers too many stories to cover all of them here, but there are some key players, characters, and some well-known stories that have even been highlighted by …. a certain superhero franchise.

- Odin - Father of the gods, ruler of Asgard, god of war, wisdom, death, and magic.
- Frigg - Wife of Odin. Goddess of love and marriage.
- Thor - Most well-known god in Norse mythology. Son of Odin. God of thunder and wielder of the hammer, Mjolnir. Protector of Asgard and Midgard (Earth).
- Loki - Half-brother to Thor. Shapeshifter and God of mischief and deception.
- Baldr -The other son of Odin. God of peace, light, nature, and beauty.
- Heimdall - Protector of Asgard.
- Hela - Goddess of Death. An odd appearance being half a beautiful girl and half a rotting corpse. She is restricted to the kingdom of the dead. She led an army of undead during Rangnarok.
- The Valkyries - minor deities that were commissioned by Odin to move the dead to the halls of Valhalla. Known to be beautiful women and fierce warriors.
- Fenrir - monstrous black wolf. He grew so large that he was considered a threat to the gods.
- Valhalla - the great hall of slain warriors. Where any warrior who dies in battle goes after they die.
- Ragnarok - a giant battle between the Aesir, or the great gods. The fight was between the gods, giants, demons, and other creatures. Only two humans would survive by hiding the World Tree and birthing the human race (very Adam and Eve type of story).

Sources for this section

1. Opera Atelier. "Mozart's Don Giovanni: A Quick Synopsis." Opera Atelier, https://www.operaatelier.com/wp-content/uploads/2024/04/OperaAtelier-StudyGuide-DonGiovanni.pdf. Accessed 7 Mar. 2024.
2. Colorado Public Radio. "Mozart's Terrifying Character in the Opera 'Don Giovanni'." CPR News, 30 Aug. 2022, www.cpr.org/2022/08/30/mozarts-terrifying-character-in-the-opera-don-giovanni/. Accessed 7 Mar. 2024.
3. Malabar LTD., https://www.malabar.net/opera/productionphotos/index.php?/category/47 Accessed 7 March 2024
4. Rush. "2112." Rush.com, www.rush.com/albums/2112/. Accessed 7 Mar. 2024.
5. The Metropolitan Opera. "Turandot." The Metropolitan Opera, www.metopera.org/discover/synopses/turandot/. Accessed 7 Mar. 2024.
6. Murashev, Alexander. "Turandot Libretto (English/Italian)." Murashev.com, www.murashev.com/opera/Turandot_libretto_English_Italian . Accessed 7 Mar. 2024.
7. Warner Classics. "Turandot - 'Nessun Dorma' (Luciano Pavarotti)." Uploaded by turecký pohodár, www.youtube.com/watch?v=cWc7vYjgnTs. Accessed 7 Mar. 2024.
8. uDiscover Music. "Nessun Dorma by Luciano Pavarotti." uDiscover Music, www.udiscovermusic.com/classical-features/nessun-dorma-pavarotti/. Accessed 7 Mar. 2024.
9. Dream Theater Wiki. "The Count of Tuscany." Dream Theater Wiki,

dreamtheater.fandom.com/wiki/The_Count_of_Tuscany. Accessed 7 Mar. 2024.

10. The Metropolitan Opera. "La Forza del Destino." The Metropolitan Opera, www.metopera.org/discover/synopses/la-forza-del-destino/. Accessed 7 Mar. 2024.

11. "IL PROGRESSIVE DEL CHIANTI CLASSICO E IL SANGIOVESE IN PUREZZA - Vinitaly 2011." Vinodaburde, https://www.vinodaburde.com/dream_theather_il_progressive_del_chianti_classico_e_il_sangiovese_in_purezza_vinitaly_2011/. Accessed 26 March 2024.

12. Kosaraju, Amrit. "The Unforgiven by Metallica." Amrit Kosaraju's Blog, amritkosaraju.blogspot.com/p/the-unforgiven.html. Accessed 7 Mar. 2024.

13. Kamiki, Yusuke, Opera Synopsis, Accessed 15 Apr. 2024, https://opera-synopsis.sakura.ne.jp/englishtannhauser.html.

14. Predota, Georg, "On This Day: 19 October, Richard Wagner's Tannhäuser Was Premiered." Interlude, Accessed 15 Apr. 2024, https://interlude.hk/on-this-day-19-october-richard-wagner-tannhauser-was-premiered/.

15. O'Dowd, Niall, "The history of whiskey in a jar." IrishCentral, Accessed 15 Apr. 2024, https://www.irishcentral.com/roots/history/history-whiskey-jar.

16. Zaleski, Annie, "The long and winding road of 'Whiskey in the Jar,' Ireland's greatest folk song." AV Club, Accessed 15 Apr. 2024, https://www.avclub.com/the-long-and-winding-road-of-whiskey-in-the-jar-iris-1798277802

17. Olsen,Bruce, Patrick Flemming, Accessed, 10/10/24, https://mudcat.org/olson/SONGTXT2.html#PATFLEM

18. Wikipedia. "The Trooper." Wikipedia, en.wikipedia.org/wiki/The_Trooper. Accessed 7 Mar. 2024.

19. Maria_Pro, The Story Behind 'The Trooper' by Iron Maiden, https://www.ultimate-guitar.com/articles/features/the_story_behind_the_trooper_by_iron_maiden-69589, Accessed 6 March 2024

20. Poetry Foundation. "The Charge of the Light Brigade" by Alfred Lord Tennyson. Poetry Foundation, www.poetryfoundation.org/poems/45319/the-charge-of-the-light-brigade. Accessed 7 Mar. 2024.

21. Historic UK. "The Charge Of The Light Brigade." Historic UK, www.historic-uk.com/HistoryUK/HistoryofBritain/Charge-Of-The-Light-Brigade/. Accessed 7 Mar. 2024.

22. YouTube. "Iron Maiden - Run To The Hills (Official Video)." Uploaded by Iron Maiden, www.youtube.com/watch?v=-Dw99l86FQQ. Accessed 7 Mar. 2024.

23. Songfacts. "Run To The Hills by Iron Maiden." Songfacts, www.songfacts.com/facts/iron-maiden/run-to-the-hills. Accessed 7 Mar. 2024.

24. Bienstock, Richard. "Scorpions' 'Wind of Change': The Oral History of 1990s Epic Power Ballad." Rolling Stone, 3 Mar. 2015, https://www.rollingstone.com/music/music-news/scorpions-wind-of-change-the-oral-history-of-1990s-epic-power-ballad-63069/. Accessed 4 June 2024.

25. Tolkien Estate. "The Lord of the Rings." The J.R.R. Tolkien Estate, https://www.tolkienestate.com/writing/the-lord-of-the-rings/. Accessed 24 March 2024.

26. "The Silmarillion." The Folio Society, https://www.foliosociety.com/usa/the-silmarillion.html. Accessed 24 March 2024.

27. Ledzeppelin.com, "Led Zeppelin Discography.", https://discography.ledzeppelin.com/. Accessed 24 March 2024.

28. Wind Repertory Project, "Symphony I (The Lord of the Rings)." Wind Repertory Project, https://www.windrep.org/Symphony_I_(de_Meij). Accessed 24 March 2024.

29. Tolkien Gateway, "Nightfall in Middle-Earth.", https://tolkiengateway.net/wiki/Nightfall_in_Middle-Earth. Accessed 24 March 2024.

30. Tolkien Gateway, "Map of Rohan, Gondor, and Mordor." https://tolkiengateway.net/wiki/Map_of_Rohan,_Gondor,_and_Mordor. Accessed 26 March 2024.

31. Britannica, "Frank Herbert.", https://www.britannica.com/biography/Frank-Herbert. Accessed 24 March 2024.

32. "To Tame a Land." Iron Maiden Wiki, https://ironmaiden.fandom.com/wiki/To_Tame_a_Land. Accessed 24 March 2024.

33. Los Angeles Philharmonic, "A Midsummer Night's Dream." LA Phil, https://www.laphil.com/musicdb/pieces/160/a-midsummer-nights-dream. Accessed 24 March 2024.

34. Dream of Poe. "Dream of Poe." Bandcamp, https://dreamofpoe.bandcamp.com/. Accessed 24 March 2024.

35. Predota, Georg, "Greek Mythology in Music: Beethoven, Handel, Dittersdorf, Strauss, Cherubini, and Roussel." Interlude, https://interlude.hk/greek-mythology-in-music-

beethoven-handel-dittersdorf-strauss-cherubini-and-roussel/. Accessed 16 March 2024.

36. The British Museum, "Who Was Achilles?" The British Museum Blog, https://www.britishmuseum.org/blog/who-was-achilles. Accessed 16 March 2024.
37. American Symphony Orchestra, "Homer's Odyssey in Music." https://americansymphony.org/concert-notes/homers-odyssey-in-music/. Accessed 16 March 2024.
38. The National Gallery, "Titian's Bacchus and Ariadne: Notes." https://www.nationalgallery.org.uk/media/13681/notes_titian-bacchus-ariadne.pdf. Accessed 16 March 2024.
39. Shapland, Andrew, "Myths of the Labyrinth." Ashmolean Museum, University of Oxford, https://www.ashmolean.org/article/myths-of-the-labyrinth. Accessed 15 March 2024.
40. Chaliakopoulos, Antonis, "Daedalus and Icarus: A Myth of Flight and Fall." TheCollector, https://www.thecollector.com/daedalus-and-icarus/. Accessed 16 March 2024.
41. Mark, Joshua J., "The Life of Hercules in Myth & Legend." World History Encyclopedia, https://www.worldhistory.org/article/733/the-life-of-hercules-in-myth--legend/. Accessed 16 March 2024.
42. CliffsNotes, "The Odyssey at a Glance.", https://www.cliffsnotes.com/literature/o/the-odyssey/the-odyssey-at-a-glance. Accessed 16 March 2024.
43. Delgado, Daniel, "Legendary Characters from Norse Mythology." Mega Interesting, https://www.megainteresting.com/history/gallery/legendary-characters-from-norse-mythology-741590756208/2. Accessed 17 March 2024.

3.
The Concept Album

A Concept album is not a new concept. Musicians have been building them for years. In modern music, the concept album is not usually one storyline or one song but a group of songs written about the same theme or topic. This also appears in several works of classical music where the composer would pick a subject and write several pieces, like The Planets by Gustav Holst. Each section of the suite is based on a different planet. One of the most notable and famous is *Mars: The Bringer of War.*

The Planets - Gustav Holst

Written between 1914-1916, each of the movements is based on the known planets (at the time) and their astrological signs.

1. **Mars** - The Bringer of War
2. **Venus** - The Bringer of Peace
3. **Mercury** - The Winged Messenger
4. **Jupiter** - The Bringer of Jollity
5. **Saturn** - Bringer of Old Age
6. **Uranus** - The Magician
7. **Neptune** - The Mystic

Volbeat - Outlaw Gentlemen and Shady Ladies

Danish rock band Volbeat gives us a 2013 album that covers many aspects of the American Wild West. It mixes many different styles of rock, metal, rockabilly, the twang of country, with a whole lot of Western themes.

- *Let's Shake some Dust - Instrumental*
- *Pearl Heart* - Pearl Heart robs a stagecoach to get money to pay for the medicine her mother needs
- *The Nameless One* - Dying with your true love and going to meet the Devil
- *Dead But Rising* - Dying while you are away from home
- *Cape of Our Hero* - How our heroes in life can fail
- *Room 24* - Spending the night in a haunted hotel room
- *Hangman's Body Count* - waiting for the hangman to come for you

Photo Credit - volbeat.dk

- *My Body* - wanting more out of life, but your body says no
- *Lola Montez* - (Based on a real-life character) A notorious Showgirl
- *Black Bart* - (Based on a real-life character) American Outlaw
- *Lonesome Rider* - A pair of singers singing back to each other about missing each other
- *The Sinner is You* - Forgiveness Of sins
- *Doc Holiday* - A song about the famous guy, Doc Holiday!
- *Our Loved Ones* - Finding the meaning of life
- *Ecotone* - transition area between belong alone and life

Carmina Burana - Carl Orff

Carmina Burana is a collection of shorter songs all put together. Originally over 1,000 poems, Carl Orff narrowed down the music into 24 sections. Originally written in Latin, German, and medieval French, the stories featured love, nature, tales of the tavern, and many more. Carmina Burana translates as Songs of Beuren. The musical works are divided into 3 sections: Springtime, In the Tavern, and The Court of Love. The short tales were written by a group of monks who would travel and get into trouble. They would eat, and get drunk, gamble, and all the other fun things to do while you are touring Europe. There is one section that translates to *"If the whole world were mine (from the Rhine to the sea), I'd give it all up if the Queen of England would lie in my arms for one night."* The text was published in 1847, but the original poems came from the 12th century. Carl Orff discovered the text and began writing the music in 1936.

The most famous of the 24 sections is *O, Fourtuna*! It is not only the opening track for the whole suite but also really the one part that everyone knows. It has been used in countless movies, TV shows, and even commercials including that Old Spice commercial and the Australian ad for Carlton Draught beer. "*It's a Big Ad!*" *O Fortun*a translates to O Wheel of Fortune. The *rota fortunae*, or Wheel of Fortune and the Christian Church are sung in contrasting ideas - the idea of allowing fate to change your life versus aligning with God - but these ideas somehow make sense in a world of war, famine, triumph, and disease.

Queensryche – Operation Mindcrime

Thematically, *Operation: Mindcrime* addresses governmental corruption, media manipulation, addiction, exploitation, revolution, and murder. Lead singer, Geoff Tate assembled the text of the songs after hearing outrageous stories from militant Quebec separatists. Combined with subplots about heroin abuse, mind control, a priest, and a doomed romance. The story revolves around Nikki, the person whose mind is being controlled.

Track list	Storyline
1. I Remember Now 2. Anarchy-X (Instrumental)	Nikki is lying in a hospital bed, nearly catatonic. He cannot remember anything but small pieces of his past. He suddenly has a flood of memories.
3. Revolution Calling	He remembers he is a heroin addict and a would-be radical that has become disenfranchised with modern society and was manipulated into joining a secret society that wants to start a revolution.
4. Operation: Mindcrime 5. Speak	At the head of this secret organization is Dr. X who is controlling Nikki through heroin and brainwashing techniques to get Nikki to be an assassin. Anytime the Dr uses the word "mindcrime", Nikki becomes docile and controlled.
6. Spreading the Disease	One of Dr. X's associates is a priest named Father William. He offers Nikki the services of a prostitute-turned-nun, Sister Mary.
7. The Mission	They engage in sex, but Nikki starts to befriend Sister Mary and begins to question what he is doing.

8. Suite Sister Mary	Dr. X sees the threat in Sister Mary and orders Nikki to kill the Priest and Sister Mary. Nikki goes to the church and kills the Priest but cannot kill Mary.
9. The Needle Lies	Nikki and Mary decide to flee but when they go to tell Dr. X, he reminds Nikki about his addiction and that Dr X is the only one that can supply his need.
10. Electric Requiem	Nikki leaves but returns only to find Mary dead.
11. Breaking the Silence 12. I Don't Believe in Love 13. Waiting for 22 (Instrumental)	He cannot cope with the loss and the realization that he may have killed her without knowing it, and falls into insanity.
14. My Empty Room 15. Eyes of a Stranger	Police arrive and arrest Nikki for the murder of Mary and the other things he did for Dr. X. Because of his near-catatonic state, he is put in a hospital, where he starts to remember…

Das Lied von der Erde - Gustav Mahler

"If I am to find my way back to myself, I have got to accept the horrors of loneliness. I speak in riddles, since you do not know what has gone on and is going on within." - Gustav Mahler before his death in 1909.

Reproduction of a fascinating autograph draft in the form of a piano-vocal score - *https://www.omifacsimiles.com/brochures/mahler_ab.html*

In the last year of Gustav Mahler's life, he suffered the death of his eldest daughter and was diagnosed with an incurable heart ailment. He refused to just lie around and rest and instead took positions as the head conductor of both the Metropolitan Opera and the New York Philharmonic.

Mahler wrote *Das Lied Von Erde* in 1908, but would never get to hear the piece performed, as he passed away before the premiere.

- Das Lied von der Erde (The Song of the Earth):
  - Das Trinklied von Jammer der Erde (The Drinking Song of Earth's Sorrow)
    - Defiance of impending death. The chorus repeats the phrase Dark is Life, Dark is Death
  - Der Einsame im Herbst (The Lonely One in Autumn)
    - The slow movement builds to a climax of despair that descends back into weariness where all passions and hope are gone.
  - Von der Jugend (Of Youth)

- Von der Schönheit (Of Beauty)
- Der Trunkene im Früling (The Drunkard in Spring)
  - These three movements are recalling the joys of the past and youth.

- Der Abscheid (The Farewell) —
  - Schwer (Difficult)
  - Sehr Mässig (Very Moderate)
  - Fliessend (Fluently)
  - Schwer (Difficult)
  - Nicht Eilen (Do Not Rush)
  - Sehr Mässig (Very Moderate)
    - The Farewell is believed to be Mahler's greatest achievement. With texts of crushing tragedy, regret. A story of weariness both physical and emotional, embracing death, and finally an outpouring of faith in life.
    - Ending in "*Everywhere forever, and ever*"

Abigail - King Diamond

In a plotline that could be pulled directly from a horror movie, the Danish heavy metal band King Diamond gives us the 1987 album *Abigail*. While not based on a real-life event, frontman King Diamond put several real-life details into the storyline. The main plot came to King Diamond (real name Kim Bendix Petersen) in a dream during "an unusually violent storm". He wrote about 75% of the original storyline the next morning after the storm, then added several sections later. The date used in the album is 7 July 1777 (or 7/7/77). The date came from a photo of a gravestone that someone had sent King Diamond. The gravestone was of a child who had lived a very short life and died on that date. While the story itself is not based, it is a collection of horrors and sadness.

King Diamond on stage in 2023. Photo Credit - metalinjection.net

- Track List
    - Funeral
    - Arrival
    - A Mansion in Darkness
    - The Family Ghost
    - The 7th Day of July 1777
    - Omens
    - The Possession
    - Abigail
    - Black Horsemen

Storyline from user brierly4 on steemit.com

- Abigail tells the story about a young couple, Miriam Natias and Jonathan La'Fey, who move into an old mansion that La'Fey inherited. It takes place in the summer of 1845. At their arrival, they are warned by seven horsemen not to move into the house because if they do "18 will become 9." They do not heed the warning and proceed to move into the mansion. During their first night, Jonathan meets with Count La'Fey, the Family Ghost, who is a deceased relative. The ghost shows him a casket in which the corpse of a stillborn child, Abigail, rests. The ghost informs him that Miriam is carrying the spirit of Abigail and that the child will soon be reborn. He insists that Jonathan must kill Miriam at once to prevent the rebirth.

- The narration then relates the story of what happened to the Count and his wife: on 7 July 1777, the Count had discovered his wife had been unfaithful to him and was pregnant with an illegitimate child. Enraged, he threw the countess down the stairs, breaking her neck and causing the child to be stillborn. The Count had the body of the countess cremated, and the stillborn fetus he named Abigail and had been mummified and laid to rest in a sarcophagus, the Count having an inexplicable urge to preserve Abigail for the future.
- The narration then returns to the summer of 1845, during which Jonathan and Miriam are beset by a range of omens; the church bell rings despite nobody being inside to ring it, flowers die, unwholesome stenches fill the house and in the dining room the table is discovered set for 3. In one incident, an empty cradle is discovered by Jonathan swaying in the air, with both him and Miriam insisting that they didn't bring it with them. The next day, Miriam is clearly pregnant, and the fetus develops quickly; Jonathan realizes that the family ghost was speaking the truth. The fatal crisis begins when Jonathan accuses Abigail of possessing Miriam, and Abigail (through Miriam) admits it. Jonathan is terrified and considers getting a priest to exorcize Miriam - Miriam, however, exercising a moment of control, urges him to cast her down the stairs to kill her just as the Count had slain the Countess and Abigail's original incarnation. Therefore, Jonathan pretends to give in to Abigail's demands, and suggests to Abigail (once she regains

control of Miriam) that she should come down to the family crypt so she can be reborn where she died. However, as the couple stands at the top of the stairs, Jonathan is distracted, and the possessed Miriam throws Jonathan down the stairs.

- Miriam gives birth to Abigail but dies shortly afterward, her last sight being of Abigail's "yellow eyes"; supposedly, her ghost can be heard screaming on the stairs in July ever after. The seven horsemen arrive at the mansion and discover the baby Abigail in the sarcophagus, eating something too horrifying for the narrator to mention (though the fact that it is found in the sarcophagus suggests that Abigail is eating her own previous body). Appalled, they take her away to bury her in a hidden chapel in the forest with seven silver spikes driven through her body (burial heard as the intro to the album), in the hope that this will prevent a further resurrection.

  - Abigail 2: The Revenge - Released 2002

    - The plot correlates with that of the original album Abigail, and the listener discovers that she is actually the half-sister of O'Brian (the mysterious leader of the Black Horsemen from the original album) and is kept alive by his intervention (the Horsemen having originally planned to nail her into a coffin with silver spikes to prevent her emerging again). The year is 1863, and Abigail has just turned 18 years old.

Ruy Blas - Felix Mendelssohn

Ruy Blas, a five-act historical drama from 1838, is a long, dark, convoluted, and implausible theater piece that exemplifies why Victor Hugo's (of Hunchback of Notre Dame fame) original stage works rarely make it to the stage anymore. It was originally commissioned by the Theater Pension Fund to write a piece based on the Hugo poem. Mendelssohn wasn't thrilled about the subject but wanted to help the organization. He wrote the song over just 3 weeks, then composed the

Overture in just 3 days, handing the final piece to the musicians just before the final dress rehearsal.

The plot has to do with a wicked, exiled nobleman who, to get revenge against the Queen who banished him, tricks her into marrying his servant Ruy Blas, whom she dubs a Duke and named prime minister. When the trick is revealed, the Queen is forced to deny the low-born Ruy Blas, even though she actually does love him. Ruy Blas responds by running a sword through the evil nobleman and then finishing himself off with a cup of poison, an act the Queen so admires that she promises to hold him in the highest esteem as she moves on with her life.

Still Life - Opeth

Still Life is the fourth studio album from Swedish progressive death metal band Opeth.

"The main character is kind of banished from his hometown because he hasn't got the same faith as the rest of the inhabitants there. The album pretty much starts off when he is returning after several years to hook up with his old 'babe.' The big bosses of the town know that he's back... A lot of bad things start happening."

Track List	Storyline
1. The Moor	Introduction to the main character. He has been an outcast for 15 years because he is an atheist. He returns to find his love.
2. Godhead's Lament	The Moor tries concealing his return. He contemplates leaving again but his desire to see his love, Melinda, outweighs any other concerns. Melinda has become a nun and finds out that he has come back.

3. Benighted	The two lovers meet in secret. The Moor tries to convince her to leave with him.
4. Moonlapse Vertigo	The Moor hides in the castle trying to plan his next move. Time is running out before someone finds him.
5. Face of Melinda	The song describes Melinda, a quiet individual who reveals she still has feelings for him.
6. Serenity Painted Death	Melinda is found out and put to death for her "unfaithfulness to God." In a fiery rage, The Moor kills all the soldiers he can before he collapses in exhaustion.
7. White Cluster	He awakens from his dream-like state to find the Council of the Cross has tried to make him repent. He refuses and is sent to the gallows. Right before he is hung, he feels Melinda's hand, welcoming him to the afterlife.

Crack The Skye - Mastodon

The band Mastodon could be included in this section for most of their albums. The 2004 *Leviathan* is based on the classic novel Moby Dick. Their 2006, *Blood Mountain* album is about getting lost on a mountain and all the crazy stuff that can happen to you while you are starving and hallucinating. But the 2009 album *Crack the Skye* comes with a far more interesting narrative. Firstly, it was an outlet for drummer Bran Dailor to deal with the suicidal death of his 14-year-old paraplegic sister, Skye. But the full story of the album is a far deeper and spiritual journey.

The story for *Crack the Skye* starts with a paraplegic boy who is having an out-of-body experience. He is traveling on the astral plane through outer space. He comes too close to the sun and burns his golden umbilical cord. He is now floating, detached. He gets sucked into a wormhole and ends up in the spirit realm and talks to spirits. The spirits tell him that he is not really dead, and they send him to a Russian cult where they decide to put him inside another body, Grigori Rasputin. *Yeah, that infamous Russian crazy man who couldn't be killed.* Rasputin is featured on the album cover.

In the story, Rasputin goes to overthrow the Russian Czar and gets murdered (as happened in real life). The two souls then leave Rasputin's body through a "crack in the sky(e)". Rasputin becomes a wise man in the story who leads the child back to his parents because they have now found him and believe he is dead. The child needs to get back to his body before it's too late. On the way back, they run into the Devil who tries to pull their souls down to hell. The story ends on a cliffhanger, not resolved.

Tracklist

1. Oblivion
2. Divinations
3. Quintessence
4. The Czar
5. Ghost of Karelia
6. Crack the Skye
7. The Last Baron

Sabaton - all their stuff…

The Swedish Power metal band Sabaton was originally formed under a different name but changed to Sabaton the year 2000. They come from Falun, Sweden that is steeped in history, including a UNESCO World Heritage Site at the mine near the city. Everything about the band, the albums, the songs are all about history. Even the space where the band started rehearsing was an old schoolhouse named Valhalla. The band's name *Sabaton,* comes from the name of the foot of a suit of armor.

On the band's website, can be found a large video library about historical events, mostly wars and battles. There are currently over 100 videos in their library. Everything about this band is history. One just needs to read the album's titles to see the connections to history.

- Stories from the Western Front (2023) - Stories from WWI
    - 1916
    - Great War
    - Price of a Mile
    - Fields of Verdun
- Heroes of the Great War (2023) - Stories from WWI
    - A Ghost in the Trenches
    - Last Dying Breath
    - The Unkillable Soldier (Lieutenant Colonel Carton de Wiart)
    - 82nd All the Way
- Steel Commanders (2021 - Single) Fighting with tanks
- Defense of Moscow (2021 - Single) Victory Day for Russia when they defeated Germany in WWII
- Royal Guard (2021 - Single) - Swedish Royal Guard, one of the oldest military regiments in the world.
- Carolus Rex (2012) - story of the Swedish empire from 1611 to the collapse under the reign of King Charles XII
    - The Lion from the North

- A Lifetime of War
- 1648
- Killing Ground

Everything that Sabaton writes and does is about history and trying to tell stories through their music. And speaking of songs and albums about war, there is a very well-known song that is not only about war but it includes the cannons.

1812 Overture -Tchaikovsky

In the year 1812, Napoleon led the French army across the Neman River, from current-day Poland into Russia. It was a disaster from the start. Even with more than 500,000 men, the French army could not move forward. The roads in Russia were in poor condition and the armies could not get supplies into the country. No one anticipated or trained for the very harsh Russian winters. The invasion only lasted six months, with a loss of over 300,000 men. Only one actual battle occurred. The Battle of Borodino lasted 1 day, and 70,000 men lost their lives across both sides. The French eventually had to admit defeat. The harsh Russian winter proved too much, and the French Army retreated. This led to the first time Napoleon was exiled to the island of Elba (which does make for the great crossword puzzle answer).

In 1880, Pyotr Ilyich Tchaikovsky was asked to produce a piece of music celebrating Russia's defeat of the French. Tchaikovsky was already a celebrated composer at this time, having already completed *Piano Concerto No.1*, *Francesca da Rimini*, *Swan Lake*, and many others. He seemed a perfect fit to compose a piece for a celebration that was due to happen in 1881. Tchaikovsky resisted, as he was not interested in a piece of music "*that was made to order*." He was originally offered three options to write, none of which Tchaikovsky wanted to do. In July 1880, Tchaikovsky wrote *'There is nothing more antipathetic to me than composing for the sake of some festivities or other. What, for instance, might one write on the occasion of the opening of an exhibition apart from banalities and generally noisy passages?' He added, however, 'I do not have it in my heart to refuse such a request,'* He completed the whole Overture, a roughly 16-minute piece of music, in less than a week. Even opting to make his writing easier by inserting sections of the French national anthem into multiple sections of the overture.

The piece has become a fundamental part of many celebrations around the world, including the United States' Independence Day celebration (The United States celebrates its Independence Day using a Russian victory song? That's odd.) The original Overture includes Cannons! Near the end of the piece, there are 16 cannon shots. In early recordings and performances, the cannon fire proved to be a logistical problem as actual cannons could not be brought on stage for a live performance. Directors often opted for something less exciting by either leaving the cannons out or going with a harmless air-rifle sound - *Pffi*! It wasn't until the 1950s, when cannon fire could be recorded off-site then played back during performances, that the cannon fire became a staple during performances.

There was a breakthrough in 1954 for a performance with the Minneapolis Symphony Orchestra. They recorded cannon shots using a small French bronze cannon on the grounds of West Point Academy, along with the 74-bell carillon (group of tuned bells) from the nearby church. These recordings took multiple takes and the locals kept phoning the academy with concerns about the noise. This performance became the standard of how to perform and/or record the 1812 Overture, which can still be heard today.

Author's Note - The 1812 Overture has always held a special place in my music heart. The first time I heard a recording with the cannons, I fell in love with it. I would practice directing it, even though I had no idea what I was doing. If you listen to the piece of music, ALWAYS listen to the full piece, not just the Finale. It is also one of the few pieces of music on my bucket list that I never got to play in all my years playing in concert bands. I did get to play Light Cavalry

Overture, also a very cool piece, but it doesn't have cannons. During the research of this book, I was disheartened to find out that Tchaikovsky was never a fan of the song and rarely spoke of it again after completing it.

Sources for this section

1. Classic FM, "Gustav Holst's 'The Planets' - An Astronomical, Mythological and Musical Guide." https://www.classicfm.com/composers/holst/pictures/holsts-planets-guide/venus/. Accessed 17 March 2024.
2. Bowar, Chad, "Volbeat, 'Outlaw Gentlemen & Shady Ladies' - Album Review." Loudwire, loudwire.com/volbeat-outlaw-gentlemen-shady-ladies-album-review/. Accessed 08 Mar 2024.
3. Stevenson, Cait. "O Fortuna: The Story of One of the Great Poems and Songs of the Middle Ages." Medievalists.net, www.medievalists.net/2019/09/o-fortuna-the-story-of-the-one-the-great-poems-and-songs-of-the-middle-ages/. Accessed 09 Mar 2024.
4. Classic FM. "The Story Behind Orff's Carmina Burana." Classic FM, https://www.classicfm.com/composers/orff/. Accessed 09 Mar 2024.
5. Libbey, Ted, NPR. "Carmina Burana: Music of Monks and Drunks." NPR, www.npr.org/2011/07/18/103529038/carmina-burana-music-of-monks-and-drunks. Accessed 09 Mar 2024.
6. Wiederhorn, Jon, uDiscover Music. "Queensrÿche's 'Operation: Mindcrime' - Review." uDiscover Music, www.udiscovermusic.com/stories/queensryche-operation-mindcrime-review/. Accessed 09 Mar 2024.
7. Last.fm. "Queensrÿche - Operation: Mindcrime." Last.fm, www.last.fm/music/Queensr%C3%BFche/Operation:+Mindcrime/+wiki. Accessed 09 Mar 2024.
8. Los Angeles Philharmonic. "Das Lied von der Erde." LA Philharmonic, www.laphil.com/musicdb/pieces/290/das-lied-von-der-erde. Accessed 09 Mar 2024.

9. Reference Recordings. "Mahler: Das Lied von der Erde." Reference Recordings, referencerecordings.com/recording/mahler-das-lied-von-der-erde/. Accessed 09 Mar 2024.

10. Steemit. "The Story of Abigail as Told by King Diamond." Steemit, steemit.com/music/@brierly4/the-story-of-abigail-as-told-by-king-diamond. Accessed 10 Mar 2024.

11. Titus, Christa, Billboard. "Things You Didn't Know About King Diamond's 'Abigail' Album." Billboard, www.billboard.com/music/rock/king-diamond-abigail-album-things-you-didnt-know-6700344/. Accessed 10 Mar 2024.

12. Alleva, Dan, "King Diamond on 2023 Tour: 'We Are Building Something That You Will Never Have Seen on a Stage Before'." Metal Injection, https://metalinjection.net/news/king-diamond-on-2023-tour-we-are-building-something-that-you-will-never-have-seen-on-a-stage-before. Accessed 24 March 2024.

13. San Francisco Symphony. "Mendelssohn - Ruy Blas Overture, Opus 95." San Francisco Symphony, www.sfsymphony.org/Data/Event-Data/Program-Notes/M/Mendelssohn-Ruy-Blas-Overture-Opus-95. Accessed 10 Mar 2024.

14. Evanston Symphony Orchestra. "Mendelssohn: Goaded by Speed in Composing the Overture Ruy Blas." Evanston Symphony Orchestra, www.evanstonsymphony.org/content/mendelssohn-goaded-speed-composing-overture-ruy-blas. Accessed 10 Mar 2024.

15. Malvern Books. "Crack the Skye." Malvern Books, malvernbooks.com/tag/crack-the-skye/. Accessed 10 Mar 2024.

16. Sabaton Official Website. "Sabaton Facts." Sabaton.net, www.sabaton.net/facts/. Accessed 11 Mar 2024.

17. Sabaton Official Website. "Sabaton History." Sabaton.net, www.sabaton.net/sabaton-history/. Accessed 11 Mar 2024.

18. Norris, Geoffrey, Gramophone. "Tchaikovsky's 1812 Overture: The Complete Guide." Gramophone, www.gramophone.co.uk/features/article/tchaikovsky-s-1812-overture-the-complete-guide. Accessed 11 Mar 2024.

19. National Geographic Education. "Napoleon Invades Russia." National Geographic, education.nationalgeographic.org/resource/napoleon-invades-russia/. Accessed 11 Mar 2024.

4.
Raging Against the Machine

The political world and the musical world have often collided. Some people think musicians should make music and stay out of politics. Some musicians believe they should use their platform to inform and inspire the world about political oppression. You can form your own opinion about this. This chapter certainly leans into the latter option. This chapter discusses the songs and bands that have used music as a venue to inform, try to persuade people, and call out issues in the world. This is nothing new.

Rage Against the Machine

One great example is Rage Against the Machine. Rage has always had a hand in a political message. In fact, most of their music has some version of a political overtone. During the 2020 United States Presidential election process, the Republican party would hold rallies and would often use songs from Rage Against the Machine during the rally. The band found out and responded nicely with a formal letter asking them to "stop using our music during your rallies. You are the reason our band exists." The Republicans stopped using their music.

There was also an exchange between guitar player Tom Morello and a "former" fan on social media. The "former" fan of Rage took to social media to complain about Rage's political opinions. "*I used to be a fan until your political opinions came out. Music is my sanctuary and the last thing I want to hear is political BS when I'm listening to music.*" Tom Morello's response was quick and on point. "*What music of mine were you a fan of that DIDN'T contain 'political BS'? I need to know so I can delete it from the catalog.*" Clearly the fan had not actually paid attention to Rage's lyrics before this.

Rage has a long history of politics and activism. On Rage's first album was the song *Killing in the Name Of* which is a direct protest song talking about police brutality. Rage shut down Wall Street during a music video shoot in the year 2000. While trying to shoot the music video for the song *Sleep Now in the Fire*, the band members were eventually arrested for disturbing the peace. The band had applied for and received permits to shoot the video on the steps of Federal Hall in New York City but were denied sound permits, so they could shoot video but no sound. They decided to start playing the music and eventually got shut down by NYC police. They agreed to "shut down" the production, which led them to grab their gear, run across the street to the steps of Wall Street, and then start playing and filming again, without a permit. The police were forced to intervene. The band kept filming as long as possible. Due to the disturbance outside, Wall Street trading was suspended for a while. The song for the music video they were trying to film, *Sleep Now in the Fire*, was written about American Capitalism, and they were more than happy to stop capitalism from moving, if only for a short time.

Again, in the year 2000, Rage Against the Machine saw more political controversy. At the 2000 National Democratic Convention, being held in Los Angeles, the band was allowed to host a concert across the street of the Convention, in protest of the US two-party system. During the concert, singer Zach De La Roca stated, "*Brothers and sisters, our democracy has been hijacked. We have the right to oppose these motherf*ckers*." The crowd eventually started turning violent and had to be dispersed by police. Six people ended up getting arrested.

There are several other examples of Rage writing songs about politics and activism.

Bulls on Parade - an indictment of the US Military complex

Freedom - calls for the freedom of imprisoned Native American leader Leonard Peltier

People of the Sun - an informative video about the people of the Zapatista revolution in Mexico

Guerrilla Radio - the exploitation of garment workers

Megadeth

Rage Against the Machine is certainly not the only heavy metal band to try to tackle politics in their lyrical message. Megadeth nearly started a riot in Northern Ireland. In a song that ended up being written after the band was quickly escorted off stage by armed protection onto a bullet-proof bus, singer and writer Dave Mustain of Megadeth wrote the song *Holy Wars...Punishment Due.*

Mustain's grandmother was from County Cork in southern Ireland, but Mustain knew nothing about the conflict between the Catholics and Protestants of Ireland and Northern Ireland when the band performed in Northern Ireland in 1988. In the afternoon before the concert, a fan was busted for selling bootlegged band t-shirts to raise money for "the cause." The band was informed about this, not knowing "the cause" was the IRA, or Irish Republican Army (from Ireland, not Northern Ireland). On stage, Mustain said before playing a cover of the Sex Pistols song, *Anarchy in the UK, "This song is for the Cause - Anarchy in Antrium."* Mustain inadvertently insulted the members of the (Northern Ireland) audience, showing support for the IRA. As Mustain said, "*After I said that, things went really fast, and I don't remember what happened.*" The next morning, after everyone had sobered up, he received the whole story about what he had done and the holy war that had been going on in Ireland for years. He then penned the song *Holy Wars...Punishment Due.*

This was not Megadeth's first foray into political statements. A song on their previous album, it has become one of the most iconic heavy metal songs ever written. The song is *Peace Sells... but Who's Buying*? While the story behind *Peace Sells* doesn't really come from an event, its message certainly speaks to politics. *Peace Sells* is CNN as seen through the eyes of a street punk.

System of a Down

While intentional or not, Megadeth has addressed some political views in their music. Another band that is steeped in politics is System of a Down. All the members of System of a Down are of Armenian descent, either born to or immigrated from the region. System's lead singer, Serj Tankian, was born in Beirut, Lebanon after his family immigrated. All four of his grandparents are survivors of the Armenian genocide that took place between 1890 and 1910. His family moved to Los Angeles when he was seven and he attended an Armenian school, where he met his future bandmates.

System of a Down's lyrics have always been politically charged. Off their first album came *P.L.U.C.K.* or Politically Lying, Unholy, Cowardly Killers. System's second album begins with *Prison Song*.

System of a Down didn't stop there. Their 2005 album brought us *B.Y.O.B.* or *Bring Your Own Bombs*. Written about the war in Iraq, along with their earlier song *Boom!* The members of System of a Down were born into a culture that was surrounded in politics and war. They put those feelings and subjects into their lyrics, bringing knowledge and activism into music.

War is always full of politics, which becomes an easy topic to write about for musicians. Earlier in this book, we looked at stories from Iron Maiden and Sabaton about the history of war and individual stories. This chapter discusses more of the bigger ideas of the politicians and generals that send those people to war and the repercussions they cause.

Disposable Heroes - Metallica - The dehumanizing nature of war and the individual toll war takes on the people who participate in it.

War Pigs - Black Sabbath - warmongering politicians who use the poor as chess pieces became the focal point of the story.

Mandatory Suicide - Slayer - about kids being drafted and sent to the front lines

These are several examples of heavy metal bands using their lyrics to delve into the world of politics and protest conflict. Wars and politics have always been around, and musicians have long used music as an outlet.

Finlandia - Sibelius

The name alone certainly does not evoke images of politics or war, but Finlandia certainly has its origins in political protest. The song itself starts in a very ominous, dark theme (dare I say Heavy Metal-esque?) and slowly adds strings and woodwinds and becomes a very bright, festive, almost nature-themed song. Written by Jean Sibelius in 1899, it is by far his most well-known piece of work. Sibelius was a native of Finland and wrote *Finlandia* for the Finnish Press Pension Celebration in 1899. On the surface, the event was like any other national celebration. In reality, it was a rally to support the freedom of the Finnish Press. At the time, Russia controlled the newspaper. The event was created to grow local support to remove Russian control.

Symphony No. 11, The Year 1905 - Shostakovich

Hey look, another song about Russian control and politics...Primering in 1957, Dmitri Shostikovich wrote *Symphony No. 11* about the Russian Revolution in 1905. The song was received with much controversy. Audiencces loved the musical piece. They felt it captured the mood, struggles, and hope of a nation during a large political event. Audiences felt it was a fitting tribute to those who had died during the Revolution. The backlash came from Russian authorities. They accused Shostikovich of showing the world about the Tsarist-style of violence that happened, which it did. Shostikovich himself clarified that he used the symphony to show feelings of fear, despair, and hopelessness and that it was a dedication to the people that died and suffered.

The piece is done in four movements: *Palace Square*, *The Ninth of January*, *Eternal Memory*, and *Tocsin*. *Palace Square* is a prelude to the horrific events that were about to take place. *The Ninth of*

January marks a massacre that happened in St. Petersburg. *Eternal Memory* reflects on the aftermath, paying homage to those people who lost their lives. Lastly, *Tocsin* is a call to action and concludes the symphony with a sense of triumph.

While audiences loved the piece, Russian authorities did not. In so much that they forced Shostakovich to join the Communist Party three years after the symphony premiered. Some say he was tortured into the decision. Some say he was blackmailed. At the time, Nikita Khrushchev created the Russian Composers Union, giving Russian composers a place to thrive, but to be a member of the union, you had to be a member of the Communist Party. Shostakovich was offered the position of General Secretary of the Union but forced to join the party.

Speaking of Nikita Khrushchev, in 1956, he wrote a report called "*On the Cult of Personality and Its Consequences*." It was a sharp criticism about the style of leadership seen in Joseph Stalin. In 1987, Guitarist Vernon Reid and singer Corey Glover from the band Living Colour were trying to fit a guitar riff with some appropriate lyrics. They had a notebook of written lyrics that were waiting for music. In that notebook was the line "cult of personality" taken from the Khrushchev report. The song is written about the duality of man and what good people and bad people have in common. The song would go on to become the band's defining moment and the riff became one of the most iconic rock riffs ever written.

William Byrd - Protestant Reformation

In 1517, Martin Luther nailed a page to the door of a church, thus starting the Protestant Reformation. This was the beginning of the idea that church and government should be separated. These same principles ended up in the United States Constitution. But the European areas became divided between political parties that agreed or disagreed with the Reformation. William Byrd somehow bridged that gap.

In this time, music was mostly written for church purposes. Operas did not exist yet, until 1597. Music was for religious purposes, not entertainment. In 1558, Queen Elizabeth I was crowned and tried to undo what her sister Mary had done with religion in England. Queen Elizabeth became "the first Protestant" and put in religious requirements for the government to follow. William Byrd rebelled and wrote music for Catholic services; his verses and text were often the last words of martyred Catholics as they were put to death. Byrd was able to get away with this style of music because Queen Elizabeth liked his secular (non-religious) music, and he was a famous composer. He was able to walk a fine line between the two religious groups and created some of the most beloved music of the time.

Beethoven and Napoleon

Ludwig van Beethoven had a man-crush on the "*hero of the people,*" Napoleon Bonapart. In 1803, Beethoven completed an epic new symphony dedicated to his hero. *Eroica* or Heroic, is a roughly 45-minute symphony that was written about the great liberator of France. Beethoven admired Napoleon's free spirit and his principles of freedom. The original name of this piece of music was *The Bonaparte Symphony.*

Officially named *Symphony No. 3 in E Flat*, *Eroica* is done in four movements. The first movement, "*Allegro con brio*" takes the listener on an emotional rollercoaster through wild extremes in key signatures. The second movement, "*Marcia funebre (Adagio assai)*" This movement evokes grief and was written to evoke feelings of the state funerals that were taking place in France at the time. The third movement, "*Scherzo (Allegro vivace)*", is a contrast to the darker second movement. Beethoven gives us visions of the future, putting away thoughts of war behind him. The fourth movement, "*Finale (Allegro molto)*" is fun and games. There are dances, solos, just fun music.

To Beethoven's disgust, in late 1804, Napoleon crowned himself the Emperor of France. Angry, Beethoven took to erasing all traces of

Napoleon off of the pages of music. He pressed so hard; that it left holes in the title page. Beethoven still loved the music, and it became his favorite piece. He renamed the piece *Eroica* and changed the narrative of the music to explore what it means to be human.

Music and politics have long been intertwined. Some artists really lean into sharing a political message or calling others into activism. Other musicians write to show support or to honor certain political parties or individuals.

Sources for this section

1. Fitzpartick, Rob. "The Roots of Rage Against the Machine." NME, https://www.nme.com/blogs/nme-blogs/the-roots-of-rage-against-the-machine-767351. Accessed 8 July 2024
2. Khan, Jamie. "Rage Against the Machine Shut Down New York Stock Exchange." Far Out Magazine, Accessed 6 July 2024, https://faroutmagazine.co.uk/rage-against-the-machine-shut-down-new-york-stock-exchange/. Accessed 8 July 2024
3. Rowley, Glenn. "Tom Morello Hilariously Claps Back at Fan Who Just Realized Rage Against the Machine Is Political." Billboard, https://www.billboard.com/music/rock/tom-morello-hilariously-claps-back-at-fan-who-just-realized-rage-against-the-machine-is-political-9400915/. Accessed 8 July 2024
4. Ling, Dave. "Holy Wars... The Punishment Due by Megadeth: The Story Behind the Song." Louder, https://www.loudersound.com/features/holy-wars-the-punishment-due-by-megadeth-the-story-behind-the-song. Accessed 8 July 2024
5. Everly, Dave. "How Megadeth's Peace Sells Turned Four Thrash Metal Kids into Superstars." Louder, https://www.loudersound.com/features/how-megadeths-peace-sells-turned-four-thrash-metal-kids-into-superstars. Accessed 8 July 2024
6. Fildes, Nic. "Life of a Song: War Pigs." Financial Times, https://ig.ft.com/life-of-a-song/war-pigs.html. Accessed 8 July 2024
7. Schwarm, Betsy. "Finlandia". Encyclopedia Britannica, 17 Mar. 2016, https://www.britannica.com/topic/Finlandia. Accessed 8 July 2024.

8. "Musical Echoes of Revolution: Shostakovich's Symphony No. 11 'The Year 1905.'" Houston Symphony, https://houstonsymphony.org/musical-echoes-of-revolution-shostakovichs-symphony-no-11-the-year-1905/, Accessed 8 July 2024

9. Horowitz, Joe. "Why Did Shostakovich Join the Party?" ArtsJournal, https://www.artsjournal.com/uq/2020/05/why-did-shostakovich-join-the-party.html. Accessed 8 July 2024

10. Siegel, Alan. "Living Colour's 'Cult of Personality' Turns 30: The Legacy of an Iconic Protest Song." The Ringer, https://www.theringer.com/music/2018/5/3/17312688/living-colour-cult-of-personality-vivid-30-years-anniversary. Accessed 8 July 2024

11. Bacon, Ariel Foshay (2012) "William Byrd: Political and Recusant Composer," Musical Offerings: Vol. 3 : No. 1 , Article 2. DOI: 10.15385/jmo.2012.3.1.2 Available at: https://digitalcommons.cedarville.edu/musicalofferings/vol3/iss1/2

12. "Protestant Reformation." The First Amendment Encyclopedia, Middle Tennessee State University, https://firstamendment.mtsu.edu/article/protestant-reformation/. Accessed 7 July 2024.

5.
These go to 11

More!

If you have ever been to a heavy metal show, you know it's loud...like really loud. Ear splittingly loud. Should-have-worn-earplugs loud. And it does seem that the larger the venue, the louder the music. Outdoor venues have towers of speakers that could rival Mt. Everest or at least 40-50 feet tall. Why? Because they can! The louder, the better. It is a common practice in metal shows to add more speakers, more power, more amps, and more everything until the band can be heard in the next country. The German power metal band Rammstein once held a concert in Coventry, United Kingdom that could be heard 11 miles away. They also lit their entire stage on fire once, so they are known for taking things to the extreme.

While creating more sound for a symphony orchestra is a significantly harder task than simply turning up the knob, there were several composers and directors that tried. Fundamentally, composers had to include dynamic markings in a wide range from *pianissimo* (very quiet) to *fortissimo* (very loud) from a *pp* to a *ff*. If they wanted it louder, add more f's. Richard Wagner and Gustav Mahler went outside the norm when it came to using more instruments as well as other instruments to make the band sound louder.

Marshall Stack

The tradition of getting louder began long before Heavy Metal music. There is the infamous Marshall Stack. In 1962, the Marshall amplifier company was just getting started and created their 4x12" amp cab (amplifier cabinet) or four 12-inch speakers in one box. Many guitar players at the time were using a 2x12" cabinet. Marshall wanted to squeeze 4 speakers into the same space that 2 were using. That was it, no big bright idea, just add more speakers to the same box. The only problem was they had to redesign the cabinet to fit the amp that sat on top of it. Three years later, the first Marshall 4x12 was released. But the original 1962 customers wanted more power and more sound, including Pete Townsend, who played for the band *The Who*. They tried to make a 100-watt 8x12" cabinet but it was deemed too heavy for the road crews, so they split the box in half, and the Marshall Stack was created. The Who became the best client for Marshall, with John Entwistle (bass player) purchasing product numbers #2, #4, #7, and #8 sets and Pete Townsend buying all the ones in between. The Who went on to become one of the greatest bands ever, and everyone wanted to sound like them. The Marshall Stack became legendary.

For modern bands it is easy to get a louder sound; turn it all the way up and add more speakers. With modern technology, every instrument and musician are assigned a microphone and everything is run through amplifiers. If the mix is missing some bass, just turn it up. The joke, of course, comes from the 1984 movie *This is Spinal Tap*. The most famous scene in the movie is when the guitar player in the (fictitious) band is explaining to the director of the documentary that his amplifiers are special because "they go to 11. It's 1 more." The idea is that he had amps made that would go louder than anything else before, so he had to change the setting on the knob to 11, instead of 10. For classical composers and directors, it was not as easy.

Standard Symphony Instrumentation

A standard symphony setup and instrumentation has changed many times over the years, and can even change per song. For some songs, everyone plays. For others, all the strings and flutes play. For other songs, the basses and brass. Or some combination of any of those.

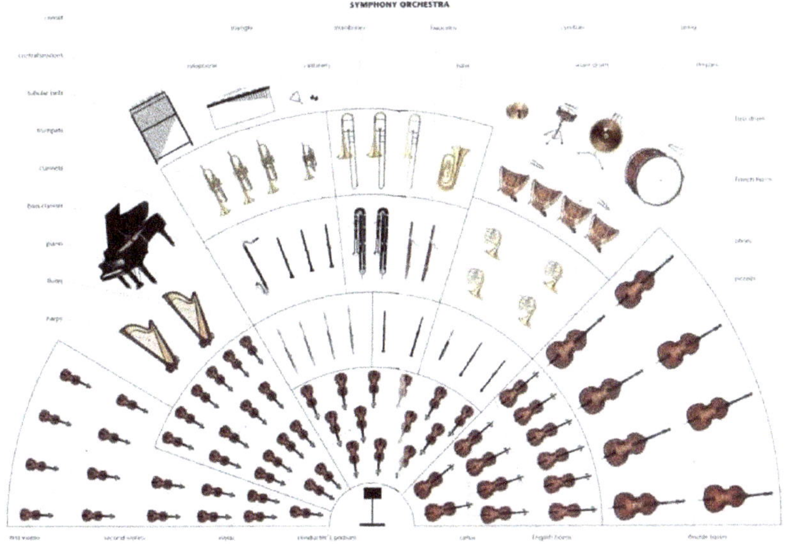

Photo Credit - pianotv.net

A full-scale symphony orchestra can consist of nearly 100 musicians

- 16-18 1st Violins
- 16 2nd Violins
- 12 Violas
- 12 Cellos
- 8 Basses
- 4 Flutes (with 1 piccolo)
- 4 Oboes (with 1 English horn)
- 4 Clarinets (with 1 bass clarinet)
- 4 bassoons
- 5-8 French Horns
- 4 trumpets
- 4 Trombones (with 1 bass trombone)

- 1 Tuba
- 1 Kettle Drum (or tympany)
- 3-4 other percussionists
- 1 harp
- 1 piano/keyboard

This setup has not always been the same. This setup has become standard in more modern times, particularly after World War II.

In any piece of classical music, the full instrumentation is as "recommended" and written for the intended parts. Directors have the option to add or subtract instruments based on what they feel would make the piece better, or they remove parts because of a lack of instrumentation (i.e.. Can't find 32 violin players)

On the other end of classical music, Mozart (~1780), for example, would write music for a small ensemble; piano/harpsichord, violin, horn, flute, harp, bassoon, oboe, clarinet and trumpet. He did have favorite instruments (*The Magic Flute*), which can be heard in different pieces. Not very large groups of instruments. He would write music according to what he wanted, not necessarily what a standard symphony setup would need.

Wagner

A classical composer who decided to change traditional instrumentation was Richard Wagner (pronounced Rick-ard Vag-ner). For example, his most famous piece *Die Walküre,* or The Valkyries, had a unique instrumentation.

Wagner Instrumentation (as played by San Francisco Symphony)

- 3 Flutes (1 on piccolo)
- 3 Oboes (1 on English Horn)
- 3 Clarinets (1 on Bass clarinet)

- 3 Bassoons
- 8 French Horns
- 4 Wagner Tubas (see below)
- 3 Trumpets
- 1 Bass trumpet
- 4 Trombones
- 1 Contrabass Tuba
- 2 pairs of timpani
- 3 Harps
- And strings…
- Singers as needed

As you can see, Wagner was bottom-loading the sound. Adding bass trumpet (*as a trumpet player, I've only ever heard of them, never played one*), 4 Wagner tubas, 1 Contrabass Tuba, and 2 sets of Timpani. A Wagner Tuba was a creation of Ricard Wagner himself. Since its birth, the Wagner tuba has been controversial as well as confusing. With the name "tuba" in the title, someone would think it is a large, deep, sounding instrument, when in reality, it fits closer to a large horn (French Horn). In size, it is about the same as a modern baritone. The notational method for the strange instrument has also confused potential composers being in B-Flat. Tubas are written in C. Invented in 1853 as Wagner was working on *Das Rheingold* and he needed the trombones to sound more like hunting horns. He invented the Wagner tuba to fill the gap between Horn and Trombone. In modern pieces, the Wagner Tuba is usually doubling the horn parts.

In Wagner, *The Ring Cycle*, he continues this pattern of using the instruments he created but adding odd and lesser-known instruments, usually on the lower end of the sound spectrum. The instrumentation for *The Ring Cycle* was close to modern symphonies of about 90 but far from normal. He also created an extension to the English Horn so it could reach a low A, called the Wagner Bell. Wagner also used A *stierhorn* (literally a steer's horn). It is an extremely long medieval bugle horn used to create sounds of the hunt. Modern symphonies use 1 harp, Wagner wanted 6 harps. And Anvils. Yes, metal anvils were used in 3 different sizes that were actually tuned to octaves of F.

Symphony of a Thousand

Unofficially called the "Symphony of a Thousand" it is actually Gustav Mahler's Symphony No. 8. He only wrote nine symphonies before his death. He was able to direct the 8th symphony just 10 months before passing away. Mahler had already established himself as a composer who would push the boundaries of traditional music.

His Symphony No. 1 had some extreme dynamic range. Really loud. Really quiet.

Symphony No 2 had a "death shriek."

The Symphony No. 3 lasted somewhere between 95 and 110 minutes. An entire concert unto itself.

No. 4 had a solo violin that was tuned a full note higher to represent Death.

No. 5 was a love letter to his wife.

The "Mahler Hammer" highlights Symphony No. 6. Anticipation builds as a literal hammer is raised high and finally dropped at the climax.

No. 7 is highlighted using a mandolin and guitar.

Symphony No. 8 was the big one. Mahler himself admitted it was something he had never written before. The story unites two poems written in two different languages, Latin and German. Movement one is highlighted with an organ that is set to a medieval Latin hymn. The second movement is themed around the last scene from Johann

Wolfgang von Gothe's play *Faust,* written in German. The structure is like that of Richard Wagner's pieces.

At 85 minutes in length, it is a hefty piece of music. It took Mahler roughly 10 weeks to compose this large symphony. His wife described his actions of writing "as if in a fever." Mahler completed the piece in September 1906, but the premiere would not happen for another four years. In early 1910, several months before the concert was to take place at a festival, Mahler had concerns that the musicians would not be able to learn their parts in time, particularly the choir. He became frantic and nearly called the whole performance off. The logistics of musicians would have been impressive.

At the direction of Mahler himself, the instrumentation calls for 171 instrumentalists and 858 vocalists. The instruments included 84 strings, 6 harps, 22 woodwinds, and 17 brass players. The extremely large choir consisted of a total of 858 singers including 350 children plus other large groups of singers from Vienna and Leipzig. The performance also included eight vocal soloists from Munich, Vienna, Frankfurt, Hamburg, Berlin, and Wiesbaden. Mahler himself wrote about the "...nearly catastrophic Barnum-and-Bailey performance." The performance finally happened at the festival in Munich. It was happily received. Mahler called it "a gift to the nation." Everyone else called it a "Symphony of a Thousand."

There have been several classical composers who have gone beyond the traditional sounds to create a different experience. Gustav Mahler created a giant symphony. Richard Wagner created his own instruments and used anvils. Modern heavy metal bands have it much easier trying to create loud sounds. Thanks to the Marshall stack, it is much easier to go to 11. Just turn up the knob one more.

Odd Instrumentation

Speaking of unique instruments used in ensembles, heavy metal has also had its fair share of unique sounds. While there is some variation, the pretty standard instrumentation for a heavy metal band is Vocals, Lead Guitar, Rhythm Guitar, Bass, and Drums.

The heavy metal world was shocked when Van Halen's 1984 record featured keyboards, particularly on the hit single *Jump*. Keyboards, or piano, have shown up in many bands, many of which fall under the Progressive Metal category like Rush or Dream Theater. Even Marilyn Manson's band has a keyboard player. Trent Reznor from Nine Inch Nails has been known to jump on the keyboard for a few songs. A few bands don't have a regular keyboardist but will feature songs with the keyboard. *Home Sweet Home* from Mötley Crüe has drummer Tommy Lee jumping behind the keys for what has become the ending song for many of their shows. Avenged Sevenfold's song *Fiction* lies heavy on the piano. Written by former drummer The Rev and finished just three days before his passing, the song features lead singer M. Shadows on piano.

While keyboards have been around and show up in many different bands and songs, there are some instruments that really stand out as "unique" to the heavy metal genre. One is the 1975 AC/DC song *It's a Long Way to the Top (If you Wanna Rock and Roll)*. Arguably one of the best rock songs ever written, it is difficult to miss the very random bagpipe breaks throughout the song. Yes, bagpipes! When producer George Young (brother to the other two guys in AC/DC) found out the lead singer Bon Scott had been in a (Bag)Pipe Band, he asked Scott to play for the track. Scott kept it to himself that he was a drummer in the Pipe Band but grabbed the bagpipes and learned to play them just for the song.

Bagpipes also show up in the popular Nu-Metal band Korn. Korn's lead singer, Johnathan Davis said in an interview that he grew up listening to bagpipes being around his grandmother, of Scottish descent, but was inspired to learn to play bagpipes after watching the end of Star Trek: The Wrath of Khan. Korn's songs that include bagpipes are *Shoots and Ladders, Lowrider, My Gift to You, Dead,* and several others.

Turntables have made their way into several bands in the heavy metal genre. Mostly started in the late 1990s with the advent of Nu-Metal, bands like Limp Bizkit, Linkin Park, Incubus, and the Deftones all have made use of a DJ and turntables. Many of these bands are known for trying to combine hip hop music and metal, so it would make sense they would incorporate a DJ. One band that doesn't combine hip-hop but certainly uses turntables is Slipknot. Syd Wilson, aka #0, has been scratching for Slipknot since nearly the beginning of the band. The songs *Spit it Out*, *Sulfur*, and *Before I Forget* and just a few that feature Syd. Slipknot also has a special instrument, perhaps not found in any other band, the beer keg. Officially listed as a percussionist, Shawn Cochran, or "Clown," is one of the founding members of the band. Clown can be seen riding high above the crowd during concerts on top of a lifted set of beer kegs, of which he plays the kegs with a baseball bat. "Percussionist."

Some other heavy metal songs that include unique instruments;

Metallica - Low Man's Lyric - Hurdy Gurdy

Metallica - Unforgiven III - Piano, Violin, Cello, French Horn

Gojira - Amazonia - Mouth Harp

Soundgarden - Spoonman - Spoons…yes, they play Spoons. The song is named after the street musician from Seattle who plays spoons, and they got him to play for the track.

Sepultura - Attitude - Berimbau - One-stringed hollowed-out gourd

There's even an entire band that uses nothing but odd instruments for a heavy metal band, and that is The Hu. Coming from Ulaanbaatar, Mongolia, the four-piece band uses traditional Mongolian instruments like the Morin Khuur (horsehead fiddle), Tovshuur (Mongolian guitar), Tumur Khuur (jaw harp), and throat singing with contemporary sounds. Starting in 2016, this group from Mongolia struggled to find their niche but released their first single and were featured by National Public Radio (NPR) in 2019.

Throughout the history of music between both classical and heavy metal, composers and bands have tried to make music louder, sound unique, and add more. Marshall made it easy for rock bands to turn up the volume. Composers like Wagner and Mahler had to find other ways to turn up the volume. They created their own instruments or simply added a giant crowd of musicians. Metal bands usually stick to the same four or five instruments but will often dabble in unique instrumentation to add different colors and sounds to a song.

Sources for the Section

1. Blabbermouth, "Rammstein's U.K. Concert Was So Loud It Could Be Heard Eleven Miles Away.", https://blabbermouth.net/news/rammsteins-u-k-concert-was-so-loud-it-could-be-heard-eleven-miles-away. Accessed 9 March 2024
2. The Idiomatic Orchestra,"Orchestra Size and Setting." https://theidiomaticorchestra.net/14-orchestra-size-and-setting/. Accessed 9 March 2024.
3. San Francisco Symphony, "Wagner: Act I of Die Walküre." https://www.sfsymphony.org/Data/Event-Data/Program-Notes/W/Wagner-Act-I-of-Die-Walkure. Accessed 9 March 2024.
4. This is Spinal Tap. Directed by Rob Reiner, Embassy Pictures, 1984.
5. "Wagner Tuba." wagner-tuba.com, https://www.wagner-tuba.com/wagner-tuba/. Accessed 10 March 2024.
6. Lyric Opera of Chicago,"Instruments of the RING." https://www.lyricopera.org/lyric-lately/Instruments-of-the-RING/. Accessed 10 March 2024.
7. Marshall, "The Story Behind the Infamous Marshall Stack." Marshall Live for Music, https://www.marshall.com/us/en/backstage/heritage. Accessed 10 March 2024.
8. Allysia, "Beginner's Guide to the Orchestra, Part 1." PianoTV, https://www.pianotv.net/2016/08/beginners-guide-orchestra-part-1/. Accessed 26 March 2024.
9. Los Angeles Philharmonic,"Symphony No. 8.", https://www.laphil.com/musicdb/pieces/4792/symphony-no-8. Accessed 1 May 2024
10. Carnegie Hall, "Mahler Symphony Cycle." https://www.carnegiehall.org/Explore/Articles/2023/07/26/Mahler-Symphony-Cycle. Accessed 1 May 2024,

11. Jomatami, "19 Metallica Songs Featuring Unusual Instruments." Ultimate Guitar, https://www.ultimate-guitar.com/news/general_music_news/19_metallica_songs_featuring_unusual_instruments.html. Accessed 17 May 2024,
12. Thehuofficial, "About." The HU Official Website, https://www.thehuofficial.com/about-1. Accessed 17 May 2024,
13. Street, Andrew P., "AC/DC's Bon Scott at 75: On the Road to His Final Success." NME, 9 July 2021. https://www.nme.com/features/music-features/acdc-bon-scott-75th-bonaversary-its-a-long-way-to-the-top-3005958. Accessed 4 June 2024
14. Downey, Ryan J. "Jonathan Davis Talks Star Trek-Inspired Bagpipes in New Korn Song." Loudwire, 5 Oct. 2021. https://loudwire.com/jonathan-davis-star-trek-inspired-bagpipes/. Accessed 4 June 2024

6.
Diabolus in Musica

Probably the single most written topic about heavy metal music. The Devil in music.

Even the band *Slayer* had an album with the same name. There is a later chapter talking about the Devil and religion in this book, but this chapter is about the sound, not the topic.

The Devil's Tritone.

In order to have a better understanding of what the devil's tritone means and why it is so famous, let's explore "regular" music and why it is more accepted.

What is a chord?

Let's see.... how far do I need to go back?

Music is made of notes or tones. If you arrange them in a nice ascending or descending order, they make a scale - Do, Re, Mi, Fa, So, La, Ti, Do.

Basic scale is a C Major Scale - C, D, E, F, G, A, B, C.

When you put the 1st, 3rd, and 5th notes of those together, they make a C Major Chord.

Songs written in C Major

- Taylor Swift - Betty
- 21 Pilots - House of Gold
- Elton John - Tiny Dancer
- The Beatles - Let It Be

As songs do not usually stay the same chord throughout, there are chord changes. Just like common scales, there are common chord changes or progressions.

There are a couple of common chord progressions based on a C Major scale.

1 -6- 4-5 or the 1st, the 6th, the 4th, and the 5th chords of the scale.

1st - C major - C, E, G

6th - Am - C - E - A

4th - C - F - 5

5th - D, G, B

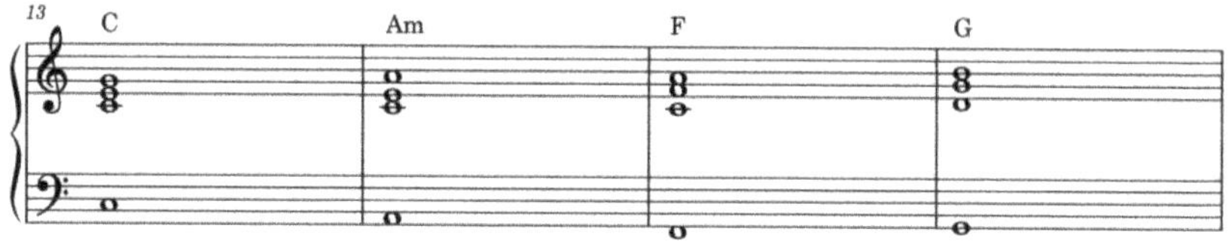

Common songs using these progressions

Journey - Don't Stop Believing

Green Day - When I Come Around

Lady Gaga - Paparazzi

Miley Cyrus - Wrecking Ball

Natalie Imbruglia – Torn

Rihanna - Take a Bow

And on…and on….and on…. So many songs. The radio hits and the Grammys would not be the same if it wasn't for this chord progression.

Why is this scale and chord so popular? Many reasons, but it begins with it's the first one that anyone learns. The scale and notes use only the white keys on a piano, making it easier to learn. C Major chord becomes the foundation for all other music theory.

Of course, there are other major scales.

D - E - F - G - A - B…. You know, right up the scale. But what happens if you don't want a Major scale?

Minor Scales

In basic theory, the difference between a Major scale and a Minor scale is not a big difference.

Below is the change of a C Major and a C Minor. You can see the 3rd, 6th, and 7th notes have been dropped by a half step.

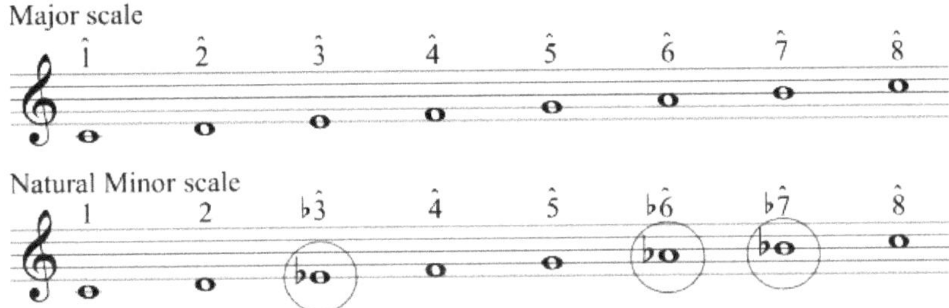

Basic theory is that music can be written in any major or minor key. But knowing how to change from one chord to another and keep the song flowing and sounding somewhat reasonable is the difficult part. This is basic music theory.

There are plenty of popular songs written in minor keys as well, just not as many.

Major key progressions are written in Uppercase - I, VI, IV, V

While minor key progressions are written in Lowercase i, v, i, iv

Black Magic Woman - Santana i, v, i, iv / i, v, i or root, 5th, root, 4th

Ain’t No Sunshine - Bill Withers i v bVII or root, 5th, flat 7th

Jolene - Dolly Parton

Another Brick in the Wall - Pink Floyd

i-VI-III-VII: A minor – F major – C major – G major

This is one of the most common minor chord progressions in all popular music. It uses chords derived only from the natural minor scale. You can hear this progression in ballads of many different genres, including hip-hop, rock, and pop. It's popular for a reason—this chord progression is emotionally resonant.

Love the Way you Lie - Eminem

Numb - Linkin Park

It is a common practice for musicians trying to create a more emotional passage or elicit a large emotional response to write a song in a minor key.

Common Minor Songs

Classical	Chord	Heavy Metal
Symphony No. 5 Beethoven *AKA Beethoven's 5th* *Prelude in C Minor* Chopin *Piano Concerto No. 1* Liszt	C Minor C, D, Eb, F, G, Ab, Bb C# Minor C#, D#, E, F#, G#, A, B	*Black Sabbath* Black Sabbath *Painkiller* Judas Priest *Rainbow in the Dark* Dio *Spiders*

		System of a Down
Piano Sonata No. 2 Chopin *Symphony No. 6 "Pathetique"* Tchaikovsky *Mass in B minor* Bach	B Minor B, C#, D, E, F#, G, A Bb Minor Bb, C, Db, Eb, F, Gb, Ab	*Fade to Black* Metallica *War Pigs* Black Sabbath *Hallowed be thy Name* Iron Maiden *Mother* Danzig
Requiem Mass Mozart *Toccata and Fugue* Bach	D Minor D, E, F, G, A, Bb, C	*Holy Wars…The Punishment Due* *Peace Sells..but Who's Buying* Megadeth *Fear of the Dark* Iron Maiden *Mr. Crowley* Ozzy Osbourne

		St. Anger Metallica
Nocturne Chopin *Piano Sonata No. 27* Beethoven	E Minor E, F#, G, A, B, C, D	*Master of Puppets* Metallica *The Trooper* Iron Maiden *Cemetery Gates* Pantera

Devil's Tritone

What does all of this have to do with the Devil? The tri-tone has been around since the Middle Ages. It was believed that the tonal interval created such a dissonant, or unpleasant sound that it was considered "the Devil's work." It was banned by the church for a while. The tritone chord lives inside every dominant 7th chord. The interval is what gives the 7th chord such a strong resolution.

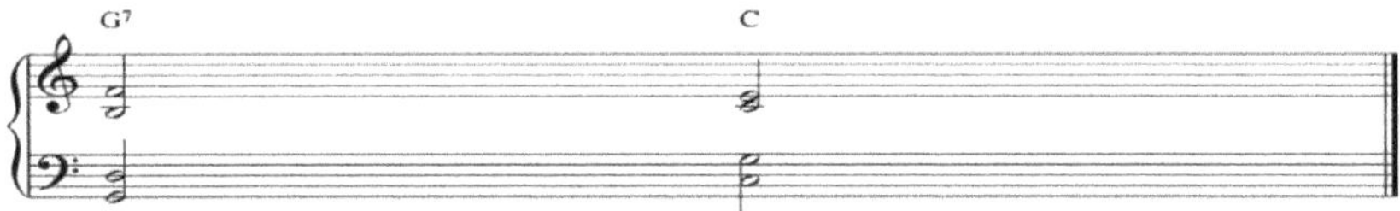

A perfect example of this theory is found in Black Sabbath's song, *Black Sabbath*. In this chord we find the interval occurs in the top 2 notes of the G7 chord. The F notes resolves (or changes) down to the E in the C Major chord, and the B resolves up to the C note.

So technically, the tri-tone is not a chord but an interval between notes. Some notes simply sound unpleasant when played together. It sounds so bad that people felt the need to name it. So bad that the church felt the need to ban music using the notes. The tri-tone simply creates a desire to resolve, or to sound better. It's the music that really leans into the tri-tone that will always sound off or "unpleasant" to some ears.

It is heavy metal's desire to create music using this dissonant tone that sets it apart from other music. The interval can be found in many different styles of music but what normally happens is there will be a minor chord with a dissonant that will then resolve to a happy, pleasant major chord. In metal music however, the dissonant interval is embraced and will often stay as an unpleasant chord.

Black Sabbath

The godfathers of heavy metal music, Black Sabbath, began a style of music that didn't even have a name. The term "heavy metal" is thought to have been coined in the Steppenwolf song, *Born to Be Wild - "heavy metal thunder"* but the term did not start getting used to describe a genre of music until later into the 1970s. Black Sabbath started in Birmingham, England. Birmingham was a factory town, and the four members of the band did not want to follow the path of factory life. They wanted to do something else. The four of them started meeting and playing music, like many teenagers do. In their downtime, they would go to the local movie theater and watch horror movies. After watching scary movies with spooky soundtracks, they had a new idea - *if people pay to watch creepy, spooky movies, wouldn't they want to pay to hear creepy spooky music?* The band started mimicking the sounds they were hearing in the horror movies and turning those into songs.

What's the best way to create creepy music? Use dissonant intervals of notes. Did Black Sabbath know they were using the Devil's tri-tone or were they just trying to create different music? Does it matter?

In addition to the band trying to create a new sound, an industrial accident helped the band more than they ever thought. Tony Iommi, the guitar player for Black Sabbath, was working at one of the many factories in Birmingham before he quit and went to music full-time. One of his many jobs was to move metal plates out of the machine after they were cut. One day, he reached in to grab the next stack just as the blade came down, cutting off the tips of 3 of his fingers. After the initial recovery time, he was afraid that he would never be able to play guitar again. His fingers were literally shorter than they used to be, so he had to learn how to play guitar differently. He actually wore false fingertips for a while after the accident to prevent his fingers from bleeding. Instead of trying to play the same way, he started experimenting with different chords and eventually created what would go on to become the foundation of heavy metal music.

It is the embracing of the minor chords and tri-tones that sets heavy metal music apart from other genres. While other bands and artists will occasionally write a song in a minor chord and then resolve the chord into a major chord, heavy metal embraces the dissonant sound.

Sources for the Section

1. Bond, Edward, "Tritone Examples." eMastered, https://emastered.com/blog/tritone-examples. Accessed 08 March 2024.
2. Longdon, Victoria, "What Is a Tritone?" Classic FM, https://www.classicfm.com/discover-music/music-theory/what-is-a-tritone/. Accessed 08 March 2024.
3. Wiederhorn, Jon, "The Devil's Chord: The Eerie History of Diabolus in Musica." Fender, https://www.fender.com/articles/chords/the-devils-chord-the-eerie-history-of-diabolus-in-musica. Accessed 08 March 2024.
4. Alves, Rui, "What Is a Tritone and How You Can Tame the Devil's Interval." Rock N' Heavy, https://rocknheavy.net/what-is-a-tritone-and-how-you-can-tame-the-devils-interval-976a359eedfe. Accessed 08 March 2024.
5. The Rolling Stone Encyclopedia of Rock & Roll. ISBN13: 9780743201209
6. Black Sabbath, "History." https://www.blacksabbath.com/history.html. Accessed 08 March 2024.
7. Downey, Ryan J. "Tony Iommi's Fingers." Loudwire, https://loudwire.com/black-sabbath-tony-iommi-chopping-fingers-off/. Accessed 09 March 2024.
8. Ultimate Guitar Tabs, https://tabs.ultimate-guitar.com/tab/. Accessed 09 March 2024.
9. Ultimate Guitar Collections, https://www.ultimate-guitar.com/collections/14173805/. Accessed 09 March 2024.
10. Boston Piano Lessons, "Pop Chord Progressions Every Pianist Should Know." https://www.bostonpianolessons.com/blog/pop-chord-progressions-every-pianist-should-know. Accessed 09 March 2024.

11. Piano for Studios, "Why Is C Major So Popular?" https://pianofs.com/why-is-c-major-so-popular/. Accessed 09 March 2024.
12. Salant, Dean, "Minor Chord Progressions." Native Instruments, https://blog.native-instruments.com/minor-chord-progressions/. Accessed 09 March 2024.
13. Pepper Rodgers, Jeffrey. "Chord Progressions in Minor Keys." Jeffrey Pepper Rodgers, https://www.jeffreypepperrodgers.com/blog/songwriting-lesson-chord-progressions-in-minor-keys. Accessed 09 March 2024.

7.
Time Signatures

Before we get into the weird songs, let's create a better understanding of what normal means. For those of you who do not play music or forgot some music basics from elementary school, let's refresh.

4/4 - When there are four notes per measure (the first 4), and the quarter note gets the beat (the second 4). This is the most common time signature in all of music, which is why it is also referred to as Common Time. Sometimes, the composer is just lazy and shows it as a big C instead of 4/4. What songs are common time, you ask? All of them…. Well, most of them. According to YouTuber and researcher David Bennett, 94% of all Pop music has a 4/4 signature. He had some theories as to why the number is that high. He thinks the preference might be built in because we have 4 arms/legs. He also theorized the preference might be cultural, as some other cultures prefer ⅞ time, like many Eastern European or Indian countries.

Let me give you some examples of popular songs in common time.

- Crazy Train - Ozzy Osbourne
- Let It Be - The Beatles
- We Will Rock You - Queen
- Firework - Katy Perry
- Yellow - Coldplay

Pretty much any pop song…and most metal songs are written in 4/4. Why? It's easy. People like to hear the easy beat. Easy to write for. There's an easy On beat or Off beat. Jazz can lay back on the 2 and 4. Rock songs land heavy on the 1 and 3. It's Common.

There are some other more common time signatures; 2/4, 3/4, 6/8.

2/4 is cut time, or half time. Literally half the counts of 4/4.

3/4 time is common waltz time. Usually, the beat will land heavier on the 1st beat.

Examples of ¾ time: Piano Man - Billy Joel, or The Waltz of the Flowers by Tchaikovsky from the Nutcracker Suite.

6/8 is 6 counts with the 8th note being the beat.

Songs in 6/8

- We Are the Champions - Queen
- House of the Rising Sun - The Animals
- From the Inside - Linkin Park
- I Put a Spell on You - Creedence Clearwater Revival
- Kiss from a Rose - Seal
- "Jesu, The Joy of Mans Desiring" (J.S. Bach)- This familiar piece is in 9/8. It sounds almost like a hurried waltz. Nine 8th notes per measure. The notes are in groups of 3, making it sound like a ¾ time.

These four-time signatures (4/4, 3/4, 2/4, 6/8) make up probably 95% of all music (just a guess). Musicians find them easy to play. Easier to direct with easy downbeats. Easy to follow for an audience. Easy to write for.

The harder time signatures usually fall outside of any of those common ones.

Asymmetrical measures. Time signatures that have an uneven number of beats.

5/4 is an example of an asymmetrical time signature. 5 notes, but the beat is still on the quarter note.

- Mission Impossible Theme is probably the most well-known 5/4 song.
- Halloween Theme (from the movie series)
- White Room - Cream
- Mars from The Planets Suite - Holst

Both classical music and metal music will often break from convention in time signatures to create a more exciting song, add struggle, change the feel, or create tension in the music. While most songs will stick to the same time signature throughout the piece, many of the examples below not only incorporate odd time signatures but change multiple times throughout a piece.

It is easy to understand in a long suite of music, like an entire opera, that the time signature would change per section of the music. Add a common time section here and put in a waltz there. In this text, we are going to look at more individual movements of music or at individual songs for their time signatures and changes.

We will start with what might be one of the most complex pieces of metal music ever written.

Dance of Eternity - Dream Theater

Above is an excerpt from measures 22 - 29 in Dream Theater's *Dance of Eternity*. There is a time signature change on every measure. This is a small example of the complexity of the piece of music. Dance was on Dream Theater's *Metropolis, Pt. 2: Scenes from a Memory* that came out in 1999. The entire album is a concept album about a man's struggle with mental health and how he is put under hypnosis. Rolling Stone magazine ranked *Metropolis* as one of the greatest metal albums ever made.

The song is only 6 minutes and 14 seconds long. There is a slight debate about the total number of time signature changes; 108, 123, or 125. Whatever the exact number is, it is well over 100 changes, and nearly every measure changes the time signature. The tempo (or speed) of the song also changes throughout, with the slowest being about 90 beats per minute and 175 beats per minute at the quickest point.

From Mike Portnoy, percussionist from Dream Theater

"...Once we got to the middle of writing the album, we decided to write the craziest instrumental song we could, and this is what we did."

"A lot of this song stems from my fascination with numbers. Many of these sections just started as a pattern of 2, then I figured do the

same pattern but with 3, then let's do 4. Then the next time through that section, let's reverse it - 4, 3, 2"

From Jordan Rudess, keyboardist from Dream Theater

"This song creates a feeling like you are skiing down a hill but you don't know how to stop."

"Several sections of this song were really me trying to show off because I had just joined the band so I was trying to impress the other guys."

Tool

Oh, Tool. Any metal fan should not be surprised that Tool is included in this section. They are known for their odd time signatures, strange sounds, unique lyrics, and amazing stage shows. It was difficult to narrow down which songs should be added to this list. I had to add a few.

Lateralus

Before we get to the time signatures, the uniqueness of this song needs to be addressed. The song is based on Fibonacci's sequence. For those not familiar, it is a pattern found in nature, in numbers, in many different things. There are some theories that the sequence drives life and nature. Numerically, the sequence builds on itself.

Photo Credit - tumamocsketchbook.com

1st number

Add the same number

Add the previous two numbers together.

Continue

1, 1, 2, 3, 5, 8, 13, 21, 34, 55, etc.

In the song Lateralus, the beginning section of the lyrics matches syllables (1, 1, 2, 3, 5, 8) to the numbers, but only goes so far, then reverses the count.

Not only do the syllables match Fibanacci's sequence, but there's also more. Maynard's vocal track starts at 1:37 into the song, or rearranged - 13:7, 13 being the 7th number of Fibonacci. There are also connections to colors and Fibonacci's sequence, but this chapter is about time signatures.

Later in the song, it does change into a more normal lyrical sequencing, but writing a song that matches and ties to a math sequence shows the high level of songwriting. Then on top of the lyrics, the band builds the song with unique time signatures, which makes sense with a numerical math pattern for the lyrics.

The song begins in a 6/8 time as it slowly builds to the guitar entrance, then switches to a repeated 9/8, 4/4, 7/8-time signature sequence. When the lyrics come in, it changes to a 5/8 time. In the 5/8 section, the drums are playing ten 1/16th notes, with the lyrics coming in;

Playing odd time signatures is difficult, even for experienced musicians. Tool certainly takes "difficulty" to a different level, crafting challenging songs to play, as well as deep meaningful lyrics that follow a specific pattern.

Schism

One of the more well-known pieces by Tool is *Schism.* The theme of the song is two lovers trying to find the pieces of their love that don't work anymore and how to fix them, the Schism between them.

In this version from *musescore.com*, the song opens in a split 5/8 and 7/8 measure. This gets repeated until after the end of the first verse, and then the Interlude switches to 6/8 and 7/8 measures. The Chorus switches to 6/4 for a few bars, then one measure of 11/8, and back to 5/8, 7/8. The Bridge of the song switches to three measures of 6/8 and one measure of 9/8, repeated 12 times. Transition out of the bridge includes a short section of 6/8 and 2/4. Then, repeated sections to the end.

There is hope if you are trying to play the piece. There is a constant beat throughout the entire piece. If you count the 8th note, it will stay constant throughout. Another way to think of these difficult time signatures is to combine them. If you put the two measures together, the 5/8 and the 7/8, it becomes a combined 12/8, or 6/4 time. The musician then visualizes the combined two measures together and it makes the phrasing a little easier to understand. Or at least it's easier to figure out how to play.

Author's note - If these two Tool songs were not enough of an experience, I would also challenge you to find the music videos for each of these songs. Not only is the listening experience a rollercoaster, but the music videos are also in a different realm. Tool's guitarist Adam Jones was a Special Effects technician and set designer for Hollywood before Tool became popular. His special effects work includes Jurassic Park, Terminator 2, and Nightmare on Elm Street 5, to name a few. Jones has directed most of Tool's music videos.

Those are a few examples of songs that are in odd-time signatures in heavy metal. Some of those songs are difficult to follow because of the odd time signature, and yet these are popular songs that fans love. The rhythms become more syncopated patterns versus traditional easy-to-follow head-banging songs. A song in common time is easy to follow, easy to find the downbeat. Easy for the audience to bounce to. Listening is easier in common time, but an odd time signature creates a more unique song.

Playing songs in odd time signatures is not someone new for a classically trained musician. Any longer piece of music is going to have time signature changes. This is a normal thing for traditional music. How often the time changes can be a difficult thing to play.

Petrushka - Stravinsky

Written in 1911, *Petrushka* is a lesser-known ballet written by Igor Stravinsky. While many people are familiar with Stravinsky's *Firebird Suite*, he did write other stuff. *Petrusky* is set in 1830s St. Petersburg, Russia. Petruska is one of three puppets of the Magician. The other two puppets are the Moor and the Ballerina. Scene 2 of the ballet is set inside Petruska's room, or her puppet box. The story shows the disdain Petruska has for the Magician and to console himself, he tries to fall in love with the Ballerina. Scene 3 takes place inside the Moor's "room." The Moor is also attracted to the Ballerina as well. Scene 4, the puppets come to life, and the Moor and Petsruka get in a duel and Petruska dies.

The music is a good mix of different styles from Russian folk songs, waltzes, and many others. With the different styles of music, the time signatures also change.

Below is an excerpt from the score of *Petruska*. For those that don't know, a score is what a conductor sees. It is all the parts of music written out, not just 1 part. This was of course, written in Russian, for Flute, Clarinet, French Horn, Cello, and Harp.

Photo Credit - imslp.org

The beginning of the pieces starts in 3/4 time, or a waltz feel. This section is part 4. Just before this part is leading from 3/4 time to 2 measures of 2/4, then back to 3/4 for 1 measure, then to this page. 7/8 - 5/8 - 7/8 - 5/8 - 8/8 (4/4). Section 4 is short but continues with this continual change in times, then goes into section 5 at a constant 2/4 time.

This is a common thing to see in larger pieces of music, some sections that change time signatures and keys many times, and others that stay constant, particularly between large sections of music. It gives the audience a feel of change, something is about to happen. In this ballet, this section comes from the opening song, which is when many things are happening. The audience sees one thing happening, and the music changes, and the audience's attention goes somewhere else to see something else happening and the music changes with the scene.

The Rite of Spring - Stravinsky

Oh, it's a song by the same guy again. One of Stravinsky's more famous songs, *The Rite of Spring* gives us some odd time signatures throughout. Another ballet composed by Stravinsky was first performed in 1913 in Paris. The premiere caused a famous scandal and ushered in a new style of music. The topic of the ballet - Pagan rituals and virgin sacrifices. Not only was the music different and the topic a bit taboo, but the choreography of the ballet was something no one had ever seen before.

There are actually two versions of this song, the original version, and then the rewritten version by Stravinsky after several performances. When he was writing Rite *of Spring*, Stravinsky was staying at a small hotel in Switzerland. He would use a piano in the hotel to help him compose. There were parts of the music he would hear in his head, but he did not know how to write them musically. Later after several performances, he rewrote those parts to make it easier for the musicians to read.

He would use very unusual time signatures like 3/16, 2/16, 2/8, 5/16, where the 16th note is the beat. He would double the note durations to make it easier to write, not necessarily easier to play.

Jesu, Joy of Man's Desiring

Even one of the most well-known pieces of music, ever written, was not written in a common time. *Jesu, Joy of Man's Desiring* has been played in so many church services all over the world, it would be impossible to count. It is used in church services, weddings, and Christmas services. Johan Sebastian Bach wrote the piece in 1723, but the original credit for the tune goes to Johann Schop who published it in 1642. Bach wrote his version of the song during his first year as musical director of the church in Leipzig, but because he finished it during Advent time, it could not be performed for a few months later.

While it doesn't change time like the other pieces we have looked at, it is certainly not a normal time. The piece is written in 9/8 time. The standard waltz is in 3/4 time. *Jesu* can be considered a lively waltz if you want to jump out of your pew and try to dance to it.

YYZ - Rush

The way home is what YYZ ment for Rush. Coming out in 1981, the band's most commercially successful album, *Moving Pictures*, included the song YYZ. The group had already been touring for several years. They would get excited when they saw the YYZ airport code on their plane ticket, as it is the airport code for Toronto, home to the band. So they made a joyful instrumental song to capture the feelings of going home after a long journey.

The opening to the song is written in 10/8 time and opens with a quick stroke pattern on the crown of the ride cymbal, then the whole band kicks in to join the odd time signature. The stroke pattern on the cymbal is not just a fun pattern, but also matches morse code…for YYZ. -.-- -.-- –.. The rest of the song then shifts to 5/8 time, a somewhat more normal time signature.

Other modern songs

There are many other examples of modern music that use odd time signatures, some of them are very well known.

All You Need is Love - The Beatles - Written in 7/4, except the chorus, and the last line of the chorus is in 6/4.

Money - Pink Floyd - also in 7/4 time

And for an odd addition…

Mario Kart 64 - Kenta Nagata - The final race results theme is in 11/8 time. You'll have to play the game to find that example.

Sources for this Section

1. Bennett, David, Why 4/4 time Dominates in Pop music, 09/28/23, Accessed 10/13/24, https://www.thomann.de/blog/en/why-4-4-time-dominates-in-pop/
2. Cunliffe, Mike, "Odd Time Signatures: Finding the Beat." Music Student 101, https://musicstudent101.com/07-odd-time-signatures-finding-the-beat.html. Accessed 27 March 2024.
3. Pattillo, Alice, "10 Awesome Metal Riffs with Odd Time Signatures." Louder Sound, https://www.loudersound.com/features/10-awesome-metal-riffs-with-odd-time-signatures. Accessed 26 March 2024.
4. Musicology, "Eternal Rhythms: Unraveling the Intricacies of Dream Theater's 'The Dance of Eternity'." Musicology, https://www.musicology.blog/eternal-rhythms-unraveling-the-intricacies-of-dream-theaters-the-dance-of-eternity/. Accessed 26 March 2024.
5. Drumeo, "The Iconic Drumming Behind "The Dance Of Eternity" | Dream Theater Song Breakdown." YouTube, uploaded by Drumeo, 25 Jan 2024, https://www.youtube.com/watch?v=49h2BivkQ0s.
6. Pianote, "The Iconic Keys Behind “The Dance of Eternity” by Dream Theater (Jordan Rudess Breakdown)." YouTube, uploaded by Pianote, 16 Feb 2024, https://www.youtube.com/watch?v=49h2BivkQ0s.
7. MuseScore, "Lateralus" by Tool. MuseScore, https://musescore.com/user/29783433/scores/6557892. Accessed 27 March 2024.
8. Drumeo, "Danny Carey: The Drumming Genius." Drumeo, https://www.drumeo.com/beat/danny-carey-genius/. Accessed 27 March 2024.

9. Sheboygan Drums, "Tool - Pneuma Drum Beat." https://sheboygandrums.com/tool-pneuma-drum-beat/. Accessed 27 March 2024.
10. Terry, "Fibonacci in Tool's Lateralus." UpVenue, https://upvenue.com/article/1142-fibonacci-in-tool-s-lateralus.html. Accessed 27 March 2024.
11. "What is the Golden Spiral? To Understand It, We Need to Draw It." Tumamoc Sketchbook, https://tumamocsketchbook.com/2021/05/what-is-the-golden-spiral-to-understand-it-we-need-to-draw-it.html. Accessed 27 March 2024.
12. Hannah, Jer. "Lateralus: A Musical Analysis." Jer Hannah's Blog, https://jerhannah.home.blog/2019/06/12/lateralus-a-musical-analysis/. Accessed 27 March 2024.
13. Reed, Ryan, "10 Things You Didn't Know About Tool's Lateralus." Revolver Magazine, https://www.revolvermag.com/music/10-things-you-didnt-know-about-tools-lateralus. Accessed 27 March 2024.
14. Musora. “Schism.” Drumeo, https://www.musora.com/drumeo/songs/schism/270769. Accessed 05 July 2024
15. Musora. “Schism.” Drumeo, https://www.musora.com/drumeo/songs/lateralus/315024. Accessed 05 July 2024
16. MuseScore, "Lateralus" by Tool. https://musescore.com/lintukoto/lateralus. Accessed 27 March 2024.
17. "Petrushka" by Igor Stravinsky. YouTube, https://www.youtube.com/watch?v=hpGYBIClZys. Accessed 27 March 2024.
18. IMSLP, Stravinsky, Igor. *Petrushka, K012.* https://imslp.org/wiki/Petrushka,_K012_(Stravinsky,_Igor). Accessed 28 March 2024.

19. San Francisco Symphony, "Stravinsky: Petrushka." https://www.sfsymphony.org/Data/Event-Data/Program-Notes/S/Stravinsky-Petrushka. Accessed 28 March 2024.
20. Los Angeles Philharmonic, "The Rite of Spring" by Igor Stravinsky. https://www.laphil.com/musicdb/pieces/4796/the-rite-of-spring. Accessed 28 March 2024.
21. Smirnov, Dmitri, "Stravinsky: Sacrificial Dance." Musical Pointers, http://www.musicalpointers.co.uk/articles/generaltopics/Stravinsky_SacrificialDance.htm. Accessed 28 March 2024.
22. Jones, Victoria Emily "The Evolution of 'Jesu, Joy of Man's Desiring'." Art and Theology, https://artandtheology.org/2017/12/17/the-evolution-of-jesu-joy-of-mans-desiring/. Accessed 28 March 2024.
23. Cook, John, YYZ and Morse Code, Accessed 10/10/24, https://www.johndcook.com/blog/2022/08/14/yyz/

8.
The Devil in I

Heavy metal music has always been associated with the Devil, Satan, and evil ideas. Yes, there are a couple of bands that practice Satanism, but the rest is all for show. The few have made a bad reputation for the rest. Heavy metal music has more ties to Christianity or any other religion.

Look at any early group photo of Black Sabbath, also known as the *Godfathers of Heavy Metal*. Many photos include members of the band wearing the crucifixes around their neck. The members of Black Sabbath always considered themselves religious. It was other people who made assumptions about their religious views based on the lyrics of the music.

Black Sabbath - Early 1970's

Photo credit -musiclipse.com/

As mentioned before, when Black Sabbath first started, they would spend extra time at the movie theater watching horror movies. The name Black Sabbath itself was inspired by a Boris Karloff movie. The music was never about worshiping the Devil. It was about making scary music. In a 2018 interview, frontman Ozzy Osbourne admitted, "*...it feels good to be bad, sometimes. I'm not bad, like, evil bad. I'm bad, in that I'm a naughty boy. I'm not a guy that worships the (expletive) devil. When Black Sabbath started, we got invited to an (expletive) graveyard at midnight. We told them: "Our (dark) image is a joke.*" In a different interview, Ozzy told a story about the time he joined a protest of his own music. There was a small group outside the venue before a concert concerned with the "Antichrist" imagery. Ozzy decided to have some fun and made his own sign with a smiley face that said, "Have a Nice Day" and joined the protest. They never knew he was there.

This same idea of a perceived "devil" has repeated itself many times throughout musical history. People make the wrong assumptions about religious alignment. When someone (or a group) does something different, they are often outcasts and sometimes accused of making a deal with the Devil. There are several examples.

Niccolo Paganini

Paganini was born in Italy in 1782 to a father who was also a musician. His father began teaching Niccolo violin at an early age and he learned quickly. After going beyond his father's abilities, he was sent to learn from better teachers. His first performance was before the age of 12. He began composing and performing, primarily in churches. At the age of 19, he was touring with his father. He had a reputation for gambling, womanizing, and alcohol. After some recovery period, he became a court violinist where his talents grew even more. He eventually began touring Europe, amassing wealth and popularity due to his ferocity and sensitivity in performance. Audiences were said to have burst into tears during the impassioned performances. Audience members began to claim that he saw the

Devil helping Paganini during the performance. The legend became that Paganini sold his soul to the devil for his extreme playing ability. The rumors became widespread. Paganini himself claimed that his talent came from his guardian angel. Whether it was true or not, it certainly did help him sell concert tickets.

Robert Johnson

Later in American history, a similar story plays out for the same reason, just with a different instrument. Robert Johnson was born in rural Mississippi in 1911, just one generation out of the abolishment of slavery. Robert grew up on a sharecropper farm and was expected to work in the fields. Instead, he took up the guitar and started writing and singing about the bitterness of oppression. After playing in small juke joints around, Robert would eventually get married. While out on tour, he learned his wife and child died during childbirth, even buried before he returned. He put his pain and passion into his music, and drove him to become a big star, only to pass away at the early age of 27 (like so many other musicians). He only recorded 29 songs that didn't really see any significant distribution until the 1950s.

But the legend of Robert Johnson has such a big place in music history. Legend says that Robert met the Devil at the intersection of 2 roads, now The Crossroads at Highways 61 and 49 in Clarksdale, Mississippi. Robert himself did nothing to stop the rumors of the legend, including writing songs about it, including "Crossroad Blues" and "Me and the Devil Blues."

The Legend - *In the delta of the Mississippi River, where Robert Johnson was born, they said that if an aspiring bluesman waited by the side of a deserted crossroads in the dark of a moonless night, then the Devil himself might come and tune his guitar, sealing a pact for the bluesman's soul and guaranteeing a lifetime of easy money, women, and fame. They said that Robert Johnson must have waited by the crossroads and gotten his guitar fine-tuned.*

Steve Vai and The Crossroads

In a strange merging of events, we can tie these stories together with the Karate Kid.

In 1986, Ralph Macchio starred in the movie *The Crossroads* which is based on the legend of Robert Johnson. The main character embarks on a journey to become a famous blues guitarist and asks for help from an old legendary blues guitarist to help him along the way. What he doesn't know is that the legend, Willie, has made a deal with the Devil.

The climax of the movie puts Eugene (Ralph Macchio) on stage in a guitar battle against Jack Butler - The Devil's Guitarist, played by virtuoso Steve Vai. Vai plays both sides of the duel for the technical aspect. Ralph Macchio just had to look good while fake playing. Steve Vai based the climaxing song of the movie on Niccolo Paganini's *Caprice #5*.

A virtuoso on guitar playing a piece that was written and performed by a virtuoso on violin.

Creeping Death

Metallica gives us one of the most religious metal songs ever written, but not based in Christian lore, but Jewish.The story of the Jewish holiday of Passover has been around...well since the Bible.

Passover is observed in the springtime to commemorate the Exodus of the Jews (Hebrews) out of Egypt. The Hebrews had settled in the land of Goshen and prospered. A new king came in, the Pharaoh, and saw the Hebrews as a problem and decided to enslave them. Still the Hebrew population grew, so the Pharaoh degreed that the first-born male of each family had to be killed in order to control the population. One Hebrew male child was saved and became the leader of the Hebrew people. His name was Moses. Moses flees the area and speaks to God through a burning bush. He is told to save the Hebrew people. He goes back to the Pharaoh and tells him to let the

Hebrews go. Pharaoh says No. Moses then sends the 10 plagues after him; turns the Nile river to blood, frogs, lice, wild animals, pestilence, boils, fire and ice, locust, darkness, and finally sending death after the first born sons of Egypt. The Hebrews marked their doors with lamb's blood so that death would pass over them.This finally convinced Pharaoh to let the Hebrews go. Moses split the Red Sea, and everyone wandered in the desert for 40 years.

Metallica captures this story in a fast-paced song off of their sophomore album Ride the Lightning. The song doesn't give all of the highlights but does tell the story from the perspective of Death, as he passes over Egypt. According to Loudersound.com, Creeping Death is Metallica's second-most played song during concerts, behind only Master of Puppets. The song has been played at over 1,600 concerts since its release in 1984.

Slayer

"F*cking SLAYER!!!" Sorry.... That is the usual response when you ask someone about the heavy metal band Slayer. Their fanbase is not only loyal but feral. I'm sure they have been voted "Most likely to have a fan carve the band's name in their arm." Yes, that happens.... often. With album titles like God Hates Us All, and song titles Evil Has No Boundaries, Hell Awaits, and Dead Skin Mask it doesn't take much to think they could be considered an evil or satanic band. And yet... Tom Araya, the band's frontman, is a practicing Catholic. The (former) drummer for the band Dave Lombardo, said in an interview that he never was a fan of some of the imagery the band promoted. Lombardo grew up with Cuban roots and his mother was a practitioner of Santeria. Lombardo never became involved and always leaned toward Catholicism. In a 2015 interview, guitarist Kerry King stated that he was not religious or a Satanist but an atheist. King - "I'm not a Satanist, I'm an atheist, but I write the best satanic lyrics on the f*cking planet. And it's great entertainment. And religion is the funnest thing to make fun of." Writing songs about Satan and religion is entertainment. It roughs peoples' feathers. Gets people to think.

Slayer has had to deal with being misunderstood their entire career. They have been called racist - even though there is a Cuban and a Chilean in the band. They were blamed for the murder of a 14-year-old girl because the boys who killed her listened to the band. They got called Nazis because (former) guitarist Jeff Hanneman had a collection of Nazi memorabilia from his father (who fought for the US in WWII). That really didn't go over well in Germany. The band was dropped from their record label because of that incident.

There have been many bands and musicians that have been wrongfully associated with the Devil's work. Some musicians enjoyed the bad press. Others have tried to distance themselves from the imagery. Does the conversation ever go the other way? Have there ever been musicians that we assumed were writing for religious purposes that had other agendas? Are there songs that we believe are church songs but have a different meaning? Were there composers who wrote music for the church but didn't follow the religion?

Ludwig van Beethoven

While nowhere as extreme an example as Slayer, Beethoven could be seen on the other side of the argument. Born in 1770 in Germany to an abusive and drunk father, Ludwig van Beethoven is one of the greatest musicians that ever lived. He wrote some of the most well-known music known anywhere. Beethoven's *5th Symphony*, *Moonlight Sonata*, *Fur Elise* just to name a few pieces. His father was the *kapellmeister,* or music leader for the electoral court. He was forced to play piano from the time he was 6. His father would severely punish him for mistakes. By the time he was 12, he was earning a living for the family writing music and playing organ.

It was assumed that Ludwig would follow in his father's footsteps as *Kapellmeister and* write music for the church. It never happened. As an adult, Beethoven was not a regular churchgoer. He even opposed the general idea of religion where regular people had to submit to a higher authority. He did not actively oppose the church, but he was just not interested. He saw the church as a means to make money, not as a moral compass.

It has been theorized that in 1819, at the age of 49, Beethoven had a spiritual crisis and began writing with a different purpose. In the same year, he wrote *Missa Solemnis,* or Solemn Mass. This is a full musical arrangement for a full-length mass, often lasting 3 hours or more. The *Missa* was mostly completed in 1822, but Beethoven worked hard to earn the most amount of money for this arrangement. After several years of negotiations, several copies were sent out, but even had to be fixed and rewritten up until his death in 1827.

Are there any pieces of classical music directly written about the Devil?

Dante Symphony

Taken directly from Dante's Divine Comedy, composer Franz Liszt created a work of music that follows Dante into the depths of Hell. Liszt began work on the epic piece of music in 1855 after his mistress introduced him to the literary work. He wanted to follow the major storyline of the tale, Inferno, Purgatorio, and Paradiso. He ended up dropping the 3rd movement on the advice of his friend, Richard Wagner. The third section of the literary text is a journey through heaven. Liszt chose to remove the 3rd movement and added a chorus of angels as a glimpse into heaven.

It took almost two years to complete the two movements. Liszt was very excited to premiere his new piece and only gave the musicians a few days of rehearsal, even though it was a difficult piece. The premiere was a disaster with musicians fumbling through trying to learn the music. The female choir lost their place and lagged behind. The poor musicianship destroyed the natural tension that was written into the music. Given more time to rehearse, the Symphony was eventually received very well and is considered one of Liszt's greatest pieces.

Danse macabre

Danse macabre, or Dance of Death, was written by Camille Saint-Saëns is one of four tonal poems written in the 1870s. The poems were inspired by examples from Franz Liszt. The text is a legend of Death dancing with a fiddle on Halloween night as skeletons dance on their graves. In a section of the music, the violin can be heard playing the devil's tritone with a diminished fifth. About midway through, the composer included *Dies irae*, a Gregorian chant theme from the Requiem Mass, or a song from the Catholic church, which is referenced by composers summoning scenes of death and judgment. Saint-Saëns put a section of church music in the middle of a song about the Devil.

On a more modern note, the metal band Ghost, released a single of the same name *Dance Macabre* in 2018. Lead singer Tobias Forge talked about how he wrote the song about the Black Death, or the plague that ran through Europe in the 1340s. People would go to the pubs and brothels and celebrate like there was no tomorrow because there often was not.

Devil's Trill Sonata

The song is officially known as the *Violin Sonata in G Minor* by Giuseppe Tartini, but better known as the *Devil's Trill Sonata*. Written well before Paganini, but certainly could have been a piece Paganini would have played. Tartini told the story of a vivid dream he had where he witnessed the Devil playing violin at a ferocious speed. What came out in the music was just a small portion of what he saw in his dream. Written about 1740, The *Devil's Trill* was Tratini's most known work.

The Devil in I

The band Slipknot gives us the title of this chapter, as well as the song that goes with it. In this chapter, we have looked at how heavy metal music, as well as others, have been viewed wrongfully based on outside opinions. Unknown guesses. Incorrect assumptions. This song is no different. It would be an easy jump to put Slipknot into a box and dismiss them based on a title like *The Devil in I.* The lyrics, on the other hand, paint a very different image. The lyrics almost read more like a sermon or as a warning. "*If you push me too far, then you'll find out what kind of person I can be.*"

The song came as part of the *.5: The Gray Chapter.* Named after co-founding member of the band Paul Gray lost his life due to an accidental overdose. Gray passed away in 2010 and the band struggled to stay together, including the founding drummer leaving in 2013. Many believe the band put more thought and heart into this album as a way to cope with losing friends and included deeper more thought-provoking lyrics than they had ever done.

The song is split in feeling; the verses are a slow melodic tempo with the vocals being featured, then the choruses are the heavy and fast up-tempo style that Slipknot is known for. With clear references to common parts of Christian church service, Slipknot makes the listener connect their own thoughts to the Devil inside themselves.

Religion has often been associated with music. Most people are familiar with the hymns and church songs. But the other side of religion can often be highlighted in many different works of music. Several musicians and bands have been mislabeled as "satanic" but are often religious themselves. God and the devil just make an interesting topic for many pieces of music across many ages.

Sources for this Section

1. Kot, Greg. "Black Sabbath." Encyclopedia Britannica, https://www.britannica.com/topic/Black-Sabbath. Accessed 10 March 2024.
2. Varga, George. "Ozzy Osbourne Talks About Life, Music, and the End of Black Sabbath." San Diego Union-Tribune, https://www.sandiegouniontribune.com/entertainment/music/sd-et-music-ozzy-osbourne-interview-20181007-story.html. Accessed 9 May 2024,
3. Grow, Kory. "Ozzy Osbourne: 5 Things We Learned From the Rocker's New Biography." Rolling Stone, https://www.rollingstone.com/music/music-features/ozzy-osbourne-things-we-learned-patient-number-9-1234590605/. Accessed 9 May 2024
4. Houston Symphony. "Paganini Theme." https://houstonsymphony.org/paganini-theme/. Accessed 10 March 2024.
5. Biography.com Editors.,"Niccolò Paganini Biography." https://www.biography.com/musician/niccolo-paganini. A&E Television Network. Accessed 10 March 2024
6. Gussow, Adam. "Blues, Bebop, and 'Race Records': Jazz in Harlem's Little Tokyo." Journal of Japanese Studies, vol. 43, no. 1, 2017, pp. 123-158. JSTOR, https://www.jstor.org/stable/10.5149/9781469633671_gussow. Accessed 10 March 2024.
7. "Robert Johnson: The Man, Myth, Legend, and Legacy." Magnolia Tribune, 13 July 2023, https://magnoliatribune.com/2023/07/13/robert-johnson-the-man-myth-legend-and-legacy/. Accessed 10 March 2024.
8. The Clark House Inn. "Crossroads." https://clarkhouse.info/crossroads/. Accessed 10 March 2024.
9. IMDb,. "Crossroads (1986)." https://www.imdb.com/title/tt0090888/. Accessed 10 March 2024.

10. chabad.org, The Passover Story in Short, Accessed 10/10/24, https://www.chabad.org/holidays/passover/pesach_cdo/aid/1827/jewish/The-Passover-Story-in-Short.htm
11. Mills, Matt, 10 Metallica songs most played live, Metal Hammer, Accessed 10/10/24, https://www.loudersound.com/features/metallica-songs-most-played-live
12. Bomb, Cherry. "Flashback: Slayer Talks About Satanism While on Tour with a Priest in 1989." Metal Injection, https://metalinjection.net/editorials/back-in-the-day/flashback-slayer-talks-about-satanism-while-on-tour-with-a-priest-in-1989. Accessed 10 March 2024.
13. Chicago Chorale. "What Is a Missa Solemnis and Why Did Beethoven Compose One?" https://www.chicagochorale.org/blog/what-is-a-missa-solemnis-and-why-did-beethoven-compose-one. Accessed 10 March 2024.
14. Dallas Symphony Orchestra. "Ludwig van Beethoven." https://www.dallassymphony.org/community-education/dso-kids/listen-watch/composers/ludwig-van-beethoven/. Accessed 10 March 2024.
15. Favorite Classical Composers. "Dante Symphony." http://www.favorite-classical-composers.com/dante-symphony.html#google_vignette. Accessed 10 March 2024.
16. Los Angeles Philharmonic."Danse Macabre." https://www.laphil.com/musicdb/pieces/284/danse-macabre. Accessed 10 March 2024.
17. Nizzat, Zailan. "Understanding Ghost's Dance Macabre." Zailanizzat.com, 21 January 2023, https://zailanizzat.com/2023/01/21/understanding-ghosts-dance-macabre/. Accessed 10 March 2024.
18. Schwarm, Betsy. "The Devil's Trill." Encyclopedia Britannica, https://www.britannica.com/topic/The-Devils-Trill. Accessed 10 March 2024.

19. Epstein, Dan. "Slipknot's '.5: The Gray Chapter': How Death and Trauma Shaped the 2014 Comeback Album." Revolver, 16 May 2019. https://www.revolvermag.com/music/slipknots-5-gray-chapter-how-death-trauma-shaped-2014-comeback-album. Accessed 23 June 2024,

9.
The Virtuosos

Throughout musical history, there have been individuals who have stood out amongst the crowd. Some of these are well-known, and some are lesser known but certainly admired among musicians. Many of these people become famous and well-known in their lifetime. Others achieve fame posthumously. The virtuosos became famous because of their musical abilities, often misunderstood as having special abilities or being really gifted. The "gift" often comes in the form of unseen years of practice, often starting at an early age.

Wolfgang Amadeus Mozart

This is an easy addition. When people think of classical music, they think of Mozart.

But why? What made him so good, and why are we still talking about him today?

If you have not seen the movie *Amadeus*, you should. Of course, the movie is based on Mozart's life, or at least the Hollywood version of the story. There is a scene in the movie where Mozart walks into the court of Emperor Joseph II of Austria while he is playing a simple march. The march had been written by the court composer, Antonio Salieri. Mozart hears the march being played badly one time by the emperor and sits down and rewrites the entire piece with much more complexity straight from memory.

Photo Credit - britannica.com

Did this event actually happen the way the movie portrayed it, or was there some free play from the writers? Whatever version of that story that happened in real life, it does show a glimpse of the genius that was Wolfgang Amadeus Mozart.

Born in Salzburg, Austria, in 1756 to a father who was also an accomplished musician. By the age of 5, Mozart could read and write music. Both of his parents put a heavy emphasis on music education for all their children. He wrote his first composition by the age of 6. Also during this same year, he was taken to the court of Vienna for his first royal concert. Ages 7, 8, and 9, his family went on a long performing tour of Europe with long stops in Paris and London. From ages 10 to 13, he was writing instrumental works in both German and Latin. In 1768, he wrote his first opera in German: *Bastien und Bastienne*. By the age of 14, he was trying to make his way as an opera writer. In Bologna, Italy, he was awarded the *Accademia Filarmonica*, even though he was well under the required 20 years of age. From age 25 until his death at 35, he lived in Vienna and wrote most of his well-known pieces. Some of his most well-known pieces came in the last few years of his life; Marriage of Figaro (1786), Don Giovanni (1787), Cosi fan tutte (1790), and the Magic Flute in 1791, the year of his death. He completed the first 2 movements of *Requiem* before his death on 5 Dec 1791.

In the 35 years of his life, he composed over 600 works of music. If you do some math, and exclude his younger years, that becomes an average of 24 works of music per year, or roughly 2 every month. That is impressive for anyone. *(It's taking me much longer to write this book)* The man understood music differently from anyone of his time.

Yngwie Malmsteen

The force that is Yngwie. Arguably, the greatest technical guitar player to come out of the 1980s heavy metal scene. He was more in love with classical composers like Bach, Beethoven, and Paganini than any of his contemporary artists. His playing style is distinctively Baroque. During concerts, he is known to wear the fancy baroque shirt to match the style of music. Yngwie rewrote the book on heavy metal guitar. If you played any one of his solos on a harpsichord, you would think it was Mozart.

Yngwie (pronounced "ING-vay") Malmsteen was born in Stockholm, Sweden in 1963. At the age of 6, Yngwie became obsessed with playing guitar after watching a television special about the death of Jimi Hendrix, including seeing him light his guitar on fire. Yngwie fell in love with the guitar playing of Richie Blackmore from the band Deep Purple, and then Yngwie's sister introduced him to the musical stylings of Bach and Beethoven. He would practice guitar until his fingers would bleed. At school he became a behavioral nightmare until his mother let him stay home to practice at the age of ten. This is also about the same time he got deep into the stylings of Paganini (see previous section) with Paganini's flair for playing, but also his wild-man image.

Photo Credit - X (Twitter) - @OfficialYJM

By the time Yngwie was 18, he had already been in and out of several bands, trying to find a sound and an audience. One of Yngwie's demo tapes ended up in the hands of American producer Mike Varney, president of Shrapnel Records, a record label already known for "shredding." Varney invited Yngwie to the United States to join the band Steeler in 1981. His first big band, Rising Force, was mostly an instrumental group giving highlight to Yngwie's playing ability, even hitting the top 60 on the Billboard chart. He even received a Grammy Nomination for Best Rock Instrumental Performance. (Heavy Metal wasn't a Grammy Category yet).

Yngwie's superfast playing style is "neo-classical." During the 1980s, he grew a decent fanbase, but it died off as many people tried to emulate his playing style. However, it was far too complex, and people were spending too much time practicing. After a car accident in 1987 that left him with severe nerve damage in his hand and another freak accident that broke his hand in 1992, Yngwie is lucky to still be playing. Time magazine listed Yngwie Malmsteen in the Top 10 Greatest Guitar players, ever (2009).

Frédéric Chopin

Frédéric Chopin.

Pronounced closer to Show-pan, not Choppin'.

Born in Poland in 1810, Chopin became a voice of an oppressed people through his music. His mother, a Polish noble, introduced him to the piano at the age of 6, and he was composing by the age of 8. He studied music in Warsaw. He had a certain ability to write music that connects traditional Polish tunes with better composition and eloquent execution. At the age of 12, he became a student of Jozef Elsner, the founder-director of the Warsaw Conservatory. Chopin started writing songs that became some of the earliest pieces in the *Romantic Era*. After planning an insurrection against the Russians

(...wait, what? Yep, he did that.), Chopin was forced to leave Warsaw for Vienna, and after fighting broke out, advised not to return.

Photo Credit - britannica.com

In 1831, he ended up in France, where he was welcomed by Polish nobility who had also been exiled. They not only appreciated his reminders of home but also paid him to teach. Chopin's Piano Sonata No. 2 in B Minor, far better known as *The Funeral March*, one of the piano repertoire's most famous works, was composed in 1837. Among the most famous of his works, which was composed late in his life, was The Minute Waltz, which was finished in 1847. Also, in 1847, he developed tuberculosis and played his final concert in front of England's Queen Victoria and writer Charles Dickens. He passed away in 1849.

Edward Van Halen

Edward Van Halen, Or Eddie, or just Van Halen. The guy who made his own guitar so he could play better.

"Van Halen changed the way electric guitarists played, the sounds they strove for, even the physical construction of the instruments they used, with multiple patents to his name. He single-handedly gave the electric guitar an extra decade or more of cultural prominence, even as he'd try to duck blame for a generation of teased-hair shredders who "played like typewriters." - Rolling Stone Magazine.

Born of a Dutch father and Indonesian mother in 1955 in the Netherlands. His family moved to California in the early 1960s. Eddie didn't speak English until he was 7 years old. Eddie and his brother, Alex, took classical piano lessons, with Eddie leaning heavily on improvisation. Eddie proved to be a quick study and stand-out student. In their teen years, Eddie switched to guitar and brother Alex switched to drums. Together they started a band called Mammoth. In 1974, they found vocalist David Lee Roth and bass player Michael Anthony and formed the band Van Halen. The band got their break in 1977 when KISS frontman Gene Simmons saw them in a club and produced their first record. The first single came out in 1978, and Runnin' with the Devil took over the world. The breakup of Van Halen in 1985 not only divided the fans but it also divided the band. They found a new singer in Sammy Hagar and the term "Van Hagar" was created. The long and sordid history of the band Van Halen could fill a whole other book (I'm pretty sure there is one…Eruption: Conversations with Eddie Van Halen)

Eddie Van Halen had an entirely new approach to traditional blues playing while modernizing it with high-speed energy. There are many different lessons to learn in the way that Van Halen plays. First, the use of vibrato. Eddie was intentional about adding vibrato, not only with the whammy bar (the long stick attached to the guitar used to bend notes) but also with his fret hand rolling back and forth to slightly change the pitch of a note. He would often use the vibrato in time with the music whereas most people will just bend a long note, Van Halen would use vibrato as another note.

Eddie would learn classic blues and speed them up at much faster tempos, to the point they do not sound like the blues but turn them into a groove. This is also the time right before a long list of bands would create the sub-genre of "Thrash Metal," which is highlighted by fast riffs. Many of these bands, including Metallica, Anthrax, Megadeth, and Slayer, were trying to copy the speed of Van Halen.

Photo Credit - Rollingstone.com

But Eddie Van Halen is most notably famous for his finger-tapping. More specifically, two-finger tapping. Tapping on a guitar string will create a short staccato note. Tapping with multiple fingers on both hands gives the sensation of incredible speed and a flood of notes coming out of the instrument. Early in his career, Eddie was known for turning his back on the crowd so that other guitar players could not see his playing technique. He created an entirely different generation of guitar players.

To go back a bit, in 1975, Eddie realized there was not a guitar on the market that was built the way he wanted or needed one. So, he built one. Dubbed the "Frankenstrat" by the fans, it became Van Halen's image. A red body with black and white stripes, this guitar and paint job became a symbol for Van Halen throughout their career. It can be seen on album covers, t-shirts, even socks. The original guitar was "retired" after 30 years of service in 2006. Eddie then played Frank2, or a replica of the original that was professionally made to his specifications by Fender but still with the classic paint job.

Sergei Rachmaninov

As far as the timeline goes, between classical music and metal music, Rachmaninov falls in between. He was born in 1873 and died in 1943. After most of the other classical musicians were gone and only just a decade after, the electric guitar was invented but not popularized. Rachmaninov had a long list of medical issues including scoliosis, *pectus excavatum*, and cardiac issues, but most notably Marfan's syndrome, which manifested in extra-large hands. One single hand could reach a twelfth, or middle C to high G. This may have accounted for his extraordinary ability to play piano.

Photo Credit - classicfm.com

Born in Oneg, Russia, just a few miles away from St. Petersburg. Sergei Rachmaninov was born into a musical family. His grandfather and father both played piano. At the age of nine, his family was forced to move to St. Petersburg, where Sergei took piano lessons at the Conservatoire. Rachmaninov's cousin, a piano player and conductor had studied in Moscow and suggested Sergei to train with Nikolai Zverev, which he did for 3 years. In 1885, he studied with his cousin Alexander Siloti and learned composition with Sergei Taneyev. He even received some advice from Siloti's friend Pyotr Ilyich Tchaikovsky. Even before his own graduation as a pianist in 1881, he composed what would become his most well-known work, *Prelude in C Sharp minor*. Upon his graduation as a composer in 1892, he was awarded a gold medal for his Pushkin opera, Aleko. The premiere of his *First Symphony* was a disaster as the conductor was drunk. Rachmaninov was so angry that he tore up the entire score. In 1893, He received an offer from Tchaikovsky to conduct his piece *The Rock*. Sadly, he never got the opportunity as Tchaikovsky passed away before any of the arrangements could be made. He then wrote *Trio élégiaque No. 2* for piano, violin, and cello as a tribute to Tchaikovsky.

He became an international figure when he conducted a concert of his orchestral works in London in 1899. He began work on his most played piece, the *Second Piano Concerto*, in 1900. In 1904, he took up a conductor's post with the Bolshoi Opera, which led him to complete two more operas, *Francesca da Rimini and The Miserly Knight in 1906.*

After the October Revolution in 1917, Rachmaninov knew he had to leave the country, so he accepted an invitation to perform in Sweden, took his family with him, and never returned to Russia. The family sailed to America in 1918, where he started many studio recordings, which are now considered some of the most valuable interpretations of not only Rachmaninov's music, but other artists as well. His last large-scale masterpiece was *Symphonic Dances* which was composed in 1940. He was gravely ill during his last recital in Knoxville, Tennessee in 1943. He returned home to Beverly Hills and passed away about a month later.

Rachmaninov's music became the inspiration for other pieces of music. During the armistice celebrations in 1918, one critic noted that he was mobbed by a group of flapper girls who wanted to hear his famous *C Sharp minor Prelude,* which then became ubiquitous in rag and jazz versions. His Symphony No. 2 was the inspiration for the 1970s song by Eric Carmen, "All by Myself." Other Rachmaninov inspirations have been Frank Sinatra's songs *Full Moon and Empty Arms*, and *I Think of You*, as well as Muse's 2001 song - *Space Dementia.*

Sergei Rachmaninov was taught and inspired by some classical composers and wrote music that became the inspiration for many modern songs.

Neil Peart

Can a drummer be a virtuoso? On our list, we have had guitar players, violin players, and piano players. Three traditional instruments for a virtuoso. I will let someone else who has far more musical knowledge debate if a drummer or percussionist can be a virtuoso, but if it is true, or allowed, Neil Peart should certainly be on that list.

The percussionist from the Canadian trio Rush, Neil Peart (pronounced PEERt, or PEER with a T on the end), is always a part of the conversation about influential drummers throughout music history. Known amongst drummers as "The Professor," he not only plays percussion but is a writer and lyricist. He was inducted into the Rock and Roll Hall of Fame in 2013. There are plenty of great drummers that are NOT in the Rock Hall, but Neil absolutely should be in there.

Born in 1952, Neil fell in love with music from a transistor radio that his parents bought him, and he started playing the drum parts with household objects. After a few piano lessons, he received a practice pad and drum lessons on his 13th birthday, which is much later in life compared to the other virtuosos on this list. He made a deal with his parents that if he stuck with the drums, they would buy him a full drum set on his 14th birthday. As you can guess, he fulfilled his side of the deal and received his first drum set at the age of 14. He also started studying under Don George. A Google search of Don George will get you to "Don George was Neil Peart's first drum teacher." In Don's own words, "*Neil didn't need another drum lesson for 30 years.*" At age 18, Neil moved to London, England, hoping to start a career as a professional drummer. Not finding work, he moved back home to Canada.

While selling tractor parts for his father, Neil auditioned to be the drummer for Rush to replace John Rutsey. The band originally formed in 1968 but needed a new drummer in 1973. According to Alex Lifeson, guitar player for Rush, commented on Neil's audition, "*he pounded the crap outta those drums. He played like Keith Moon and John Bonham at the same time.*" (Also, two other drummers that could also be included as drummer virtuosos) Neil's first gig with the band was opening for the bands Manfred Man and Uriah Heep in front of 11,000 people.

The band started producing and recording albums at a rate that few musicians could duplicate.

1974 - Rush

1975 - Fly by Night

1975 - Caress of Steel

1976 - 2112

1977 - All the World's A Stage - Live Album

1977 - Farewell to Kings

1978 - Hemispheres

1980 - Permanent Waves

1981 - Moving Pictures (by far, the largest commercial success)

1982 - Signals

Nine studio albums and a Live album in less than 10 years. Most bands today are producing albums at one or less per year, more likely one album every couple of years, and most bands never get to make more than three or four. There were a few other albums, *Presto*, *Counterparts*, and *Test for Echo,* before the band would take a hiatus due to tragedy that struck Neil's personal life.

After the 1997 *Test for Echo* tour had ended, Neil's daughter was headed back to college and was in a fatal car accident. 10 months later, Neil's wife passed away from cancer. As a way of coping with a double tragedy, Neil turned to the other focus of his life, his motorcycle. Neil was already an accomplished rider, even riding between Rush's concert stops. After losing his family, Neil spent 14 months and 55,000 miles on the road across Canada, into Alaska, down the west coast *(even through this author's city, where he described it as billboards and fast-food chains…which is accurate*) into Mexico and Belize before returning to Quebec. He put the story of his journey into a book, *Ghost Rider: Travels on the Healing Road.*

Neil returned to the drums in 2001, and the band released a new album in 2002, *Vapor Trails*. In 2015, the band started the R40 tour celebrating 40 years of the band. It would be the last tour Rush would embark on before Neil decided to retire. He was just a few months into retirement, and he began to not feel well. Neil passed away in 2020 after a 3-year battle with cancer.

Not only are Neil's performances legendary, but his drum sets themselves are a sight to behold.

Photo Credit - remo.com

Standard drum set
Snare drum 1 or 2 toms Floor tom Bass drum, operated with floor pedal Hi-hat cymbal Ride cymbal Crash cymbal
Neil Peart drum kit (example)
2 snare drums 14x6.5

13x3

4 toms

7x8

7x10

8x12

9x13

3 floor toms

12x15

13x15

16x16

Bass drum

16x23

Ride cymbal

22”

3 crash cymbals

20”

18”

16”

2 Splash cymbal

10”

8”

2 Hi-Hat

10”

8”

3 China cymbals

20”

20” Prototype

19”

Pitched cowbells

Electronic drum pad

All of that extra drum kit was not just for show. Neil would use it all. His drum solos quickly became legendary, not only for length but more for complexity. He removed the bottom skin (or head), which gave a shaper attack, but less resonance, so the sound would fade away faster. All his drums were tightly and specifically tuned. In what is Rush’s most well-known song, *Tom Sawyer*, you can hear higher-pitched drums. Those are concert-sized drums stretched higher than normal.

He also incorporated other percussion instruments into his set including woodblocks, Rototoms, octobans, chimes, timbales, tambourines, tubular bells, glockenspiels, and an occasional gong. A bit later in his career, Neil added electronic parts that included triggers, sequences, and even full electronic sections. He even experimented with different manufacturers to create different sounds. Many artists will get sponsored by a brand and stick with that one their whole career. Neil tried Rogers, Slingerland, Tama, DW, and a few others. He spent a good portion of his career with DW. There is at least 1 solo featured on every live Rush album.

It is not often that we hear that a great musician wants to get better, or actively seeks to get better. In 1991, Neil was asked to play for a Buddy Rich tribute concert. Buddy Rich was an American jazz drummer (*Caravan*) that Neil referred to as one of his influences. After the performance, Neil was not happy with the sound of the concert, so to make up for it, he produced two tribute albums to Buddy Rich, all played by the Buddy Rich band. Neil was so impressed with the band's drummer, Steve Smith, that he was inspired to reinvent himself as a jazz drummer. He studied jazz drumming under Freddie Gruber and Peter Erskine and performed another Buddy Rich show in 2008. The new jazz influence can be heard in the later Rush albums such as Test for Echo, Snakes and Arrows and Clockwork Angels.

"Peart is the thinking man's wordslinger equivalent of Yngwie Malmsteen." - Bruce Pollack.

Not only was Neil Peart the amazing drummer for Rush, but he was also the primary lyricist.

From an interview, "*Were you a student of songs before you started writing them?*"

Peart - "*No, but I was a student of words and a student of rhythm. I think as a listener of music, lyrics were strictly tertiary for me.*" Neil's theory was that if you want to look for new ideas, read a book. Neil could regularly be seen reading while on tour. The writings of Ayn Rand were the inspiration for the entire 2112 album. Samuel Taylor Coleridge's Kubla Khan comes out in *Xanadu.* Neil read several books about World War II and wrote the song *Manhattan Project*. He would also use real-life events to write many songs.

- Subdivisions - growing up in suburbia
- Spirit of Radio - the 1970s heyday of FM radio
- Countdown - Space Shuttle Columbia
- Red Barchetta - driving through the countryside

Opera Virtuosos

Since this book highlights many operas, it would be necessary to include some vocal virtuosos. There are many. Most of the ones on this list will be more modern vocalists, some are still alive. These people still follow a similar pattern as the instrumentalists; they start at an early age, have many years of practice and hard work, hundreds of performances, and slowly build a career.

Luciano Pavarotti

His role in making *Nessun Dorma* famous is already mentioned in this book. Pavarotti was already well-known in opera and classical communities long before the soccer campaign.

Born in Modena, Italy in 1935, Luciano lived there his entire life. Born into a family that was steeped in music, his father was a baker but sang in the city choir. During his teen years, Pavarotti joined the same choir. His father saw Luciano's talent early and had him learn vocals with a private tutor. At the age of 22, his mentor moved away, and Luciano quit his day job to turn towards a life of music. He won a vocal contest in 1961 which led to his operatic debut singing Rodolfo in Puccini's *La Boheme*. The same director for *La Boheme* would eventually be the same director to help Pavarotti in Milan as well as with the Metropolitan Opera in New York. Pavarotti's first recording came in 1964 with excerpts from *La Boheme*, and several other operas. From there, his reputation grew, landing parts in many other operas around the world. His first role on film came in the mid-1960s for Verdi's *Requiem*. This film performance included solos from Leontyne Price, Fiorenza Cossotto, Pavarotti and Nicolai Ghiaurov.

Photo Credit - https://www.pavarottiofficial.com/

The 1970s had Luciano at the top of his career with his United States debut with the Metropolitan Opera in 1972. Known not only for his voice and size, but his openness and generosity. The Met performance was Donizetti's *La Fille du regiment,* with Pavarotti getting 17 curtain calls (which means he was able to sing 17 times during the performance). By the 1980s, Pavarotti was a universal favorite. The 1990s brought The Three Tenors Concert tour. Los Angeles in 1994, Paris in 1998, and Yokohama in 2002. Pavarotti headlined a concert in London's Hyde Park in front of 150,000 people, even in the rain. 1993 was the Central Park concert in New York in front of 500,000 people.

Luciano Pavarotti passed away in 2007 after being forced to end his farewell tour early due to a medical diagnosis.

Maria Callas

"*One of the most iconic opera singers of the 20th century.*" - England National Opera

American by birth, but born to Greek emigrants in 1923, Maria Callas is most known for her work in Italian operas. She had several high-profile performances in Europe and the United States. Her US tour is highlighted by her 1965 performance in the opera *Tosca* with Maria in the title role.

Maria's mother moved herself and Maria back to Athens, Greece in 1937, apparently fed up with her husband's cheating. The same year, Maria began her musical education at the Greek National Observatory. She originally began as a contralto but moved to soprano. At age 18, Maria made her professional debut as Puccini's Tosca, a role that she became associated with throughout her career. During World War II, the family was struggling, and Maria's mother forced her to go out with the occupying German soldiers to get better food and money. Her relationship with her mother was never the same after that time.

At the age of 21, Maria returned to New York in 1945 with 56 performances from seven different operas. Many consider this the proper start to her career and the foundation of what would become her fame. Some other highlights during the post-war 1940s; are Ponchielli's La Gioconda in Verona, Verdi's Aida and Wagner's Tristan and Isolde, Kundry Parsifal, and even Brünnhilde from The Valkyrie.

The 1950s brought high-profile performances around the world, including La Scala, Milan, Covent Garden, London; the Lyric Theatre of Chicago; and the Metropolitan Opera, New York. Callas was often her own worst critic. She was known for withdrawing from a performance if she felt her singing was below par. She felt she did not want to disappoint the public.

The 1960s brought her most famous performance, reviving her role of Tosca. July 1965 brought her final operatic performance in Covent Garden at the age of 41. Later, Callas tried to revive a part of her career by offering masterclasses at Julliard School in New York. She also did a small tour of joint concerts in 1973 with tenor Guiseppe di Stefano. Even though they were sold out, the performances were flawed, and not at the level either artist wished they were. Callas' final recital was in 1974 as she withdrew from music completely. Living alone in Paris, she suffered a heart attack and passed away in 1977.

Placido Domingo

Not only known for his roles as an opera singer, Placido Domingo is also known as a conductor and opera administrator. As of this writing, he is set to perform in Japan in the month of May 2024. In his own words, "*If I rest, I rust.*"

Born in Madrid, Spain in 1941, Placido is the son of a baritone and soprano. Placido and his sister were often watched by aunts and uncles while their parents were away on tour. According to Placido, "*I owe my love of music to the zarzuelas I heard so often from the time I was a small boy.*" A zarzuela is a style of lyrical drama with spoken work and sung lyrics. Domingo not only loved these as a child but continued to keep the genre of music alive throughout his career. At the age of 5, his parents were asked to join a zarzuela company, tour Latin

America, then move to Mexico. At the age of eight, Placido's parents sent for their children to join them in Mexico, where he would remain until the age of 21. Any time the production company needed children; the Domingo children were called upon. This is where Placido began to learn theatrical performance. At this same time, Placido began piano lessons and was identified as a great talent. At the age of 14, his parents enrolled him at Mexico's National Conservatory. A full school to study music as well as all regular school subjects. During this educational time, Placido grew in musical knowledge, studying voice with Carlo Morelli, acting and singing in various plays and operas, appearing on Mexico's television station, and even rewriting American Pop songs into Spanish-language arrangements.

Domingo made his opera debut in 1959 at the age of 18 in a small role in the Verdi opera *Rigoletto*. Guiseppe Verdi's operas became a staple for Domingo's performances. Nearly one-quarter of all his performances throughout his career were a Verdi piece. Domingo's first leading role came two years later in *La Traviata*. Domingo has sung 26 different roles from seventeen different Verdi operas.

1965 was when Placido's career really took off when he was offered a contract with the New York City Opera, with his US debut singing parts in *Madama Butterfly*. Near his 25th birthday, Placido sang the lead role in the US premiere of Alberto Ginastera's opera *Don Rodrigo*, the role of the king of Spain. This was also the first performance at the new Lincoln Center in New York. His European debut came in 1967 performing *Tosca* with the Hamburg Opera. In the same year, he performed in Berlin, Houston, Baltimore, Lima, Santiago, Chicago, Los Angeles.

The same week that man first walked on the moon also was Domingo's debut where opera began, in Italy. Placido received the lead role of Calaf in *Turandot* in July 1969. His lead role was played opposite another very famous vocalist, Birgit Nilsson. Domingo remembers the moon showing over the open amphitheater and the chorus to the moon being particularly appropriate. Domingo made his hometown debut in Madrid, Spain in 1970.

The 1970s and 80s were a busy time for Domingo. 1972 alone had 9 debuts, 19 operas, and 4 concerts. 1973 was his debut as a conductor with the New York City Met with productions of *La Traviata* and *Il Trovatore*. He has since conducted over 300 opera and concert performances all over the world. Newsweek magazine featured Domingo on the cover and dubbed him the "King of Opera." He won his first Grammy award in 1984 for the album "*Always in My Heart*." He also appeared on the late-night show Johnny Carson and even showed up on Sesame Street. He performed a benefit concert for Pope John Paul II in 1982 and was made Commendatore of the Italian Republic by the Italian President. 1985 brought a tragedy when Domingo lost his aunt, uncle, and cousins in a large earthquake that hit Mexico City. In response, he hosts several benefit concerts to support survivors. The Mexican government awarded him the Order of the Aztec Eagle.

Possibly the performance that Placido Domingo is most well-known for is the Three Tenors concert. Already mentioned in this book, the 1990 concert took place just before the World Cup in Rome with fellow tenors Luciano Pavarotti and Jose Carreras with Zubin Mehta conducting. Creating such a stir around the world that the concert not only awarded the group a Grammy Award, then several years later, a world tour took the group to many places in 1996-97.

Domingo received the Premio Príncipe de Asturias from Spain in 1991. It is an award given to people with exceptional accomplishments in the arts and sciences. Among many other awards, he also received a star on the Hollywood Walk of Fame. In 1993, Domingo founded *Operalia*, an annual international voice competition to help grow vocal talent. From 1996 to 2003, Domingo was the Artistic Director of the Washington National Opera, based at the Kennedy Center. He was also the General director of the Los Angeles Opera starting in 2003.

At the age of 68, Placido Domingo made a shift and debuted as a baritone, instead of his usual tenor voice, with the Berlin Staatsoper, again with a Verdi opera, *Simon Boccanegra*. Originally only planning a few performances, he quickly expanded and sung about 150 opera performances as a baritone. 2009 brought an unusual prize for Domingo, the Birgit Nilsson Award after her death. She left instructions for a $1,000,000 prize to be awarded to someone who made major contributions to the world of opera. On her own instructions, Placido Domingo was the winner of the first prize given. He used the money to help support *Operalia*.

Placido Domingo is not only world-renowned for his voice in both tenor and baritone, but he has also conducted hundreds of concerts, began programs to promote music and opera, given hundreds of benefit concerts for various causes, and has received countless awards. He continues to perform and promote the arts.

Renee Fleming

"*Possibly the most beautiful soprano voice in the world.*" - Frankfurter Allgemeine Zeitung

Born in Pennsylvania but grew up in Rochester, New York Renee Fleming has become one of the most iconic modern vocalists, period. Both of her parents were singers. Her musical education included Juilliard School, degrees from Eastman School of Music, and a Fulbright Scholar in Germany. Her musical career breakthrough came in 1988 as the Countess in Mozart's *Le Nozze di Figaro*. She has had title roles in operas around the world including Desdemona in Verdi's *Otello*, Violetta in Verdi's *La Traviata*, the title roles in Dvořák's *Rusalka*, Massenet's *Manon and Thaïs* and Richard Strauss's *Arabella*, Countess Madeleine in *Capriccio* and the Marschallin in *Der Rosen-kavalier*.

She is also known as a singer willing to try new music and has premiered many newly written plays and operas with the Metropolitan Opera, Lyric Opera of Chicago, and the San Francisco Opera to name a few. Her first Grammy Award came in 1998 in the category of "Best Classical Vocal Performance." Since then, she has gone on to win five total Grammy awards with 18 total nominations.

Fleming became the first woman to solo headline an opening night gala at the Metropolitan Opera in 2008. In a historic first, in 2012, she was given the honor of performing on the balcony of Buckingham Palace in front of Queen Elizabeth II. In 2013, US President Obama awarded Renee with the National Medal of Arts, America's highest honor for an individual artist. She was the first ever classical artist to sing the Star-Spangled Banner at the Super Bowl in 2014. In 2023, she was a Kennedy Center Honoree.

Not only a musician, but Renee Fleming has also been an advocate for literacy. She has been involved in campaigns for the Association of American Publishers and the Magazine Publisher's READ poster campaign. She wrote a book called "The Inner Voice" about her career and musical process.

Speaking of great vocalists, who is the greatest heavy metal vocalist?

While there has been much debate, usually driven by personal preference, one name always comes up in the conversation.

Ronnie James Dio

Best known for being the vocalist and frontman for his own band Dio, and the replacement singer for Black Sabbath after Ozzy left, Ronnie James Dio certainly left his mark and influence across all Heavy Metal music. At only 5'4" (162cm) Ronnie was not a big frontman, but his voice was. He is also known for popularizing the famous heavy metal hand signal, the "Metal Horns" which he copied from his Italian grandmother, who would use it to ward off evil spirits.

Dio's career started with a band called Vegas Kings, then he formed Elf in 1967. That band would often open for a young Deep Purple. In 1975, Deep Purple's guitarist Richie Blackmore and Dio got together to form Rainbow and made three albums. This is where people started paying attention to Ronnie's unique, powerful rock voice. In 1979, Ronnie replaced Ozzy Osbourne in Black Sabbath and went on to make three albums with them before leaving and starting a new band under his own name, Dio. That band has gone on to sell 20 million albums worldwide.

Ronnie was also a philanthropist and would hold charity concerts for various groups. In 1985 he organized the Hear 'n Aid project, which is a charity for heavy metal bands to perform and raise money. The album that came out of the project has raised over two million dollars. Ronnie was named "Best Metal Singer" during the Revolver Golden Gods Awards in 2010, just a few months before his passing.

Rolling Stone Magazine eulogized Ronnie: "*It wasn't just his mighty pipes that made him Ronnie James Dio – it was his moral fervor.. what always stood out was Dio's raging compassion for the lost rock & roll children in his audience. Dio never pretended to be one of the kids – he sang as an adult, assuring us that we weren't alone in our suffering, and someday we might even be proud of conquering it*".

Sources for this section

1. Forman, Miloš, director. Amadeus. Performances by F. Murray Abraham, Tom Hulce, Elizabeth Berridge, Roy Dotrice, Simon Callow, Orion Pictures, 1984.
2. "Wolfgang Amadeus Mozart." Encyclopedia Britannica, Encyclopædia Britannica, Inc., https://www.britannica.com/biography/Wolfgang-Amadeus-Mozart. Accessed 24 Mar. 2024,
3. Opera Philadelphia. "Composer: Figaro." https://www.operaphila.org/whats-on/on-stage-2016-2017/figaro/composer/. Accessed 12 March 2024.
4. Jason. "Yngwie Malmsteen - Master of the Shred." GuitarSite.com. https://www.guitarsite.com/yngwie-malmsteen/.Accessed 12 March 2024.
5. Time Photo. "The 10 Greatest Electric Guitar Players." Time, 28 July 2015, https://time.com/3961025/10-greatest-guitar-players/. Accessed 12 March 2024.
6. Eddie Van Halen Eruption Solo." YouTube, uploaded by VanHalen765, 10 May 2009, https://www.youtube.com/watch?v=e7F3FoCgFvU. Accessed 13 March 2024.
7. "Frédéric Chopin." UNHCR, https://www.unhcr.org/ceu/9443-chopin-frederic.html. Accessed 13 March 2024.
8. Classics for Kids. "Frederic Chopin." https://www.classicsforkids.com/composer/frederic-chopin/. Accessed 13 March 2024.
9. Classic FM. "Frédéric Chopin: 11 Facts About the Great Composer." https://www.classicfm.com/composers/chopin/. Accessed 13 March 2024.
10. Weiderhorn, Jon, and Kory Grow. "Eddie Van Halen: 20 Essential Songs." Rolling Stone, 7 October 2020,
11. https://www.rollingstone.com/music/music-features/eddie-van-halen-tribute-1081034/. Accessed 13 March 2024.

12. Biography.com, "Eddie Van Halen." https://www.biography.com/musicians/eddie-van-halen.Accessed 13 March 2024.
13. Smithsonian Institution, "Rock 'n' Roll: Eddie Van Halen's 'Frankenstein' Guitar." National Museum of American History, https://americanhistory.si.edu/collections/nmah_1397533/. Accessed 13 March 2024.
14. Ramachandran M, Aronson JK. The diagnosis of art: Rachmaninov's hand span. J R Soc Med. 2006 Oct;99(10):529-30. doi: 10.1177/014107680609901015. PMID: 17066567; PMCID: PMC1592053.
15. Boosey & Hawkes. "Sergei Rachmaninoff Biography." https://www.boosey.com/composer/Sergei+Rachmaninoff?ttype=BIOGRAPHY. Accessed 15 March 2024.
16. Maddocks, Fiona. "Goodbye, Russia: Rachmaninov in Exile." The Guardian, 28 May 2023, https://www.theguardian.com/music/2023/may/28/goodbye-russia-rachmaninov-rachmaninoff-in-exile-fiona-maddocks. Accessed 15 March 2024.
17. MasterClass, "Rachmaninoff: A Guide to the Music of Sergei Rachmaninoff." https://www.masterclass.com/articles/rachmaninoff-music-guide. Accessed 15 March 2024.
18. Flagstaff Symphony Orchestra, "Sergei Rachmaninoff's Influence Is All Over Pop Music." https://www.flagstaffsymphony.org/concerts/sergei-rachmaninoffs-influence-is-all-over-pop-music/. Accessed 15 March 2024.
19. Classic FM,"Rachmaninov." Accessed 25 Mar. 2024, https://www.classicfm.com/composers/rachmaninov/.
20. Toews, Brandon. "Neil Peart: The Drummer's Drummer." Drumeo, https://www.drumeo.com/beat/neil-peart-genius/. Accessed 5 March 2024.

21. Rush.com, "Rush: The Band." https://www.rush.com/band/. Accessed 14 March 2024.
22. Rush Fandom, "Neil Peart Equipment." https://rush.fandom.com/wiki/Neil_Peart_equipment. Accessed 14 March 2024.
23. Wiederhorn, Jon. "Rush Drummer Breaks Silence About Family Tragedy in New Book." MTV, 5 September 2002, https://www.mtv.com/news/qt27ux/rush-drummer-breaks-silence-about-family-tragedy-in-new-book. Accessed 14 March 2024.
24. Cross, Alan. "Neil Peart: Rush Drummer Remembered by Alan Cross." Global News, 11 January 2020, https://globalnews.ca/news/6420132/neil-peart-rush-drummer-alan-cross-tribute/. Accessed 14 March 2024.
25. Peart, Neil. Ghost Rider: Travels on the Healing Road. ECW Press, 2002.
26. Pollock, Bruce. "Guitar Practicing Musician." Power Windows, October 1986, http://www.2112.net/powerwindows/transcripts/19861000guitarpracticingmusician.htm. Accessed 14 March 2024.
27. Majewski, Greg. "Five Lessons Songwriters and Musicians Can Learn from Neil Peart." DIY Musician by CD Baby, 13 January 2020, https://diymusician.cdbaby.com/music-career/five-lessons-songwriters-and-musicians-can-learn-from-neil-peart/. Accessed 14 March 2024.
28. Remo, "Neil Peart." , https://remo.com/profile/neil-peart/. Accessed 25 Mar. 2024
29. Luciano Pavarotti Official Website, "Story: Pavarotti - Part 2." https://www.pavarottiofficial.com/story-pavarotti-part-2/.Accessed 8 May 2024
30. English National Opera. "The Beginner's Guide to Maria Callas." https://www.eno.org/discover-opera/the-beginners-guide-to-maria-callas/. Accessed 8 May 2024,
31. Plácido Domingo Official Website, https://www.placidodomingo.com/. Accessed 9 May 2024,

32. Decca Classics. "Biography." https://www.deccaclassics.com/en/artists/reneefleming/biography/. Accessed 9 May 2024
33. Ronnie James Dio Official Website, "Biography." https://ronniejamesdio.com/bio/. Accessed 9 May 2024

10.
Not all songs are about Butterflies and Rainbows

While it is unclear who originally said the phrase “Not everything is about butterflies and rainbows.” It does appear in many songs, quotes, and signs on walls. The phrase's meaning is always the same. Yes, there are great things in life that make us happy, but not everything is great. There is always a balance. If you have great things, there must be bad things.

Earlier in this book, God and the Devil were discussed. It is easy to find the yin and yang, the light and dark about that conversation. But there is the other side of life that has little to do with religion but is still not goodness in this world. Music can be an outlet for writers to express their feelings and emotions. Artists can put their pain into their music. This idea has always been in music. But it is the darker side that is embraced by heavy metal music that draws some fans. People can go through rough times in their life. If they hear a song that they connect to, it can be liberating, cathartic, and healing.

This is your trigger warning - we are going to jump right into some dark stuff.

Cue the sad, gloomy music.

Suicide

Suicide has always been a big subject for musicians. Depression, of course, goes right along with the thoughts of suicide. Death in general is a sad subject, but someone contemplating killing themselves is a dark subject.

Fade to Black - Metallica

Written as a literal suicide note, Metallica's 1984 song *Fade to Black* was oddly received by the critics. Metallica established themselves as a Thrash band from their debut album, *Kill 'em All,* in 1982. Speed and volume were the band's norm. This was the band that went faster than everyone else and melted faces. Then they came out with their sophomore album *Ride the Lightning* in 1984 and released a single that starts as a ballad with acoustic guitars?? It confused so many people, but the fans reacted to it as it was a subject few artists at the time were talking about.

The producer of the album was not worried about the fans liking the song. He knew that Fade to Black was not "thrashy", but it was dark. James Hetfield, singer and songwriter wrote the song after the band's equipment trailer had been stolen. All of the band equipment was gone. This happened right before they were to leave for Denmark to record the album. They ended up recording on borrowed equipment late at night when no one else was scheduled in the studio. The minor acoustic guitar riffs are arpeggios. Apparently, the same sad arpeggios that James would play after the equipment was stolen.

Hungarian Suicide Song

Hungary is known for a few things that are dark: evil dictators and fascism to name a couple. One dark connection to Hungry comes with a long story that is *Gloomy Sunday,* aka *The Hungarian Suicide Song.* Written during the Great Depression in 1933, composer Reszõ Seress wrote the song as a plea for mercy as the world was at its worst. Written in a minor key, of course, the tune is ominous but catchy.

The song gained in popularity in 1941 after it was recorded by popular jazz singer Billie Holiday. This recording became the most popular version of the song ever recorded. The song has also been recorded by Sinead O'Connor, Mel Tormé and Sarah Vaughn, but never as popular as the Billie Holiday version.

There is a certain lore surrounding the song. Like the popular horror movie *The Ring*, if you listen to the song many times you are more likely to commit suicide. The song has been attributed to a large body count. There are several stories that are hard to confirm.

- A shoemaker whose suicide note quoted the song.
- A girl in Vienna drowned while holding the sheet music for the song
- A man who shot himself after telling loved ones the song wouldn't leave his head
- A woman in London who overdosed while listening to "Gloomy Sunday"
- Sheet music was found in the apartment of a shopkeeper in Berlin who hanged herself
- And many, many more

There are two parts to the story of this song that are particularly compelling. During the 1980s, Hungary had one of the highest suicide rates in the world. But perhaps the most tragic is that the author himself died after jumping off of a building in 1968. Due to good reasons, the Hungarian authorities supposedly discouraged the broadcast of the song.

Suicide Note Part 1 & 2 - Pantera

This song could fit this category of suicide as well as the next about drug usage, as *Suicide Note parts 1 and 2* were written by lead singer Phil Anselmo after he had overdosed on heroin and was clinically dead, then revived. The lyrics follow the author's challenges of drug use and giving up.

Parts 1 and 2 were tracks 6 and 7 off Pantera's popular 1996 album *The Great Southern Trendkill*. The very heavy part 2 is a big contrast to the ballad style of part 1. Part 1 is the story of a man at his lowest point describing what is going through his head during drug use, as he contemplates suicide, again, after already attempting to slit his wrists. Part 1 features a 12-string acoustic guitar. Part 2 is a fast-paced nightmare with screaming vocals and whammy effects. Part 2 lyrics focus around ending your life by a self-inflicted gunshot.

Pathetique - Tchaikovsky

While this is a debated topic, Tchaikovsky's *Symphony Number 6*, also known as *Pathetique,* is considered his suicide note. The piece was written near the very end of his life. Tchaikovsky conducted the premiere of the piece just nine days before he passed away. It is commonly accepted that Tchaikovsky died from catching cholera by drinking unboiled water. And according to official records, that is what happened. But it is also well known that he was in a very dark place in his life. Tchaikovsky was a very emotional person. He was known to be a neurotic, highly sensitive person, full of phobias. He had a phobia that his head would fall off when he was conducting. It was also rumored that he had a homosexual relationship with a young nobleman, and that story was about to be exposed. This would have brought public shame and destroyed his social status. This was Russia in the late 1800s after all.

Fourth Piano Sonata - Prokofiev

Sergei Prokofiev wrote many pieces of music during his time as a composer. But it is perhaps his 2nd Piano Sonata that comes from the darkest place. Prokofiev was just about to graduate from the St. Petersburg Conservatory. He has become great friends with Maximilian Schmidthof. The two shared common interests and Max was an inspiring composer, like Prokofiev. Max was a deeply troubled person and in 1913, took his own life. He left behind a suicide note for Sergei that simply stated, "*I am writing to tell you the latest news, I have shot myself...The reasons are unimportant.*"

After some time Segeri dedicated his new piano sonatas to Maximillian, as Sergei had already shared sections of the pieces with him. The Sonata was first performed on February 5, 1914, with

Prokofiev on the piano. The audience reaction was extremely mixed. Some cheered. Some "hissed like cats." Some were simply frozen with fright at the ferocity at which Prokofiev attacked the piano. A few years later, the original score of the music was destroyed by a fire due to the revolution. Prokofiev was able to recreate most of the work from memory and notes. A friend of his who was able to hear both the old and the new versions said it never was the same.

Inside the Fire - Disturbed

In a 2008 interview with FaceCulture.com, David Draiman, lead singer and writer of the band *Disturbed,* talks about how he wrote the song *Inside the Fire*. The song was written about his girlfriend, Devon, while they were teenagers. His heroin-addicted girlfriend took her own life due to the couple breaking up. The song was written as Draiman remembers the last image of her open casket, and him having a vision of the Devil on his shoulder, trying to convince him to take his own life to be able to be with her again. Draiman had nightmares of this vision for years following. He recalls believing the relationship only delayed the inevitable, that his girlfriend was bound to have a hard life.

On the other side of the tragedy of suicide, songwriters can put their pain into a positive message. David Draiman and the other members of Disturbed have lost many friends due to suicide, overdoses, and other tragedies. They started a "Fighter of the Month" club, highlighted on their website, where fans of the band can nominate a friend or loved one who is struggling with depression, PTSD, fighting cancer, or anything of that nature. The "Fighters" can then get support from the other fans of the group and share experiences. Also, during concerts, the band will bring fans on stage and let them tell their story of struggle to the audience to share their support.

Disturbed has also written several songs of hope and light to spread a positive message. "*The message for 'The Light' is one of positivity*," admits Draiman. *"Most people are quite apprehensive about the "dark" periods and experiences of their lives. However, sometimes those dark periods of time are a necessary path we must take in order to finally see 'the light,' so to speak.*"

Leave a Light On - Papa Roach

In a very recent collaboration, Aug 2024, Papa Roach took on the topic of suicide. Papa Roach teamed up with country music artist Carrie Underwood to record the song *Leave a Light On (Talk Away the Dark)*. Papa Roach originally wrote the song in 2022 on their album *Ego Trip*. The lead singer for Papa Roach connected with Underwood to record a version that would try to connect with a wider range of audience, sharing both metal and country music fans. The duo partnered with American Foundation for Suicide Prevention (AFSP) and all proceeds from this single will go to help that organization.

The song itself is written as a plea from a concerned friend talking to someone, they are worried about. The concerned person sees their friend in a dark place and wants to help them and to try to get them to talk about their dark thoughts. Singer and frontman, Jacoby Shaddix and Carrie Underwood wanted to raise awareness about suicide prevention and mental health.

Drug Use

Master of Puppets

The imagery on the album cover is that of puppet strings attached to burial crosses. This image sets up the title track to Metallica's third album *Master of Puppets*. The song is a cautionary tale about drug use and free will.

Image Credit - discogs.com

The drug of choice in this case is cocaine. The song was released in 1986 as the United States was being overrun by cocaine use. Alcohol was the preferred vice of the band, hence the band's nickname during this time, *Alcoholica*. Drummer Lars Ulrich admitted to cocaine use during this time to keep up with the other guys drinking and having fun. Lars would get drunk faster than everyone, so to keep up with them, he turned to cocaine.

The lyrics are written from the perspective of cocaine itself being the master of the user. It is really about how things get switched and the drugs start controlling you, not you controlling the drugs.

"*The guitar is a great way to channel your anger and frustration into something positive.*"

James Hetfield, singer and guitar player for Metallica

Symphonie Fantastique - Berlioz

Hector Berlioz was a little crazy. Hector Berlioz was REALLY into opium.

Many people enjoyed opium in the 19th century for medical purposes. Hector Belioz had his share of medical problems, but he took opium to a different level. The fact he was already a little crazy didn't help his addiction. For example, Berlioz became engaged to a lady named Camille Molke. While he was away in Italy, he received a letter from Camille telling him that she was breaking off the engagement. Fueled by opium, Berlioz then concocted a plan to not only murder Camille, but also her new boyfriend and Camille's mother. He purchased a pair of pistols for the event and poison as backup. He went as far as purchasing a maid's outfit as a disguise to get into Camille's house. His plan was called off during his return trip to France, as he realized he had left the maid outfit in Italy. He was a little crazy.

Photo Credit - theclassicalgirl.com

In a strange irony, Berlioz wrote *Symphonie Fantastique* about a completely different woman. Harriet Smithson was a Shakespearean actress who performed Hamlet in 1827. Berlioz saw the production and became smitten with Harriet. He began stalking her. He would send her letters and flowers, even renting an apartment near hers to keep tabs on her. Naturally, Harriet was concerned by his behavior and rejected him. He retreated and wrote *Symphonie Fantastique.*

Upon hearing the symphony, Harriet realizes the music is written about her and she falls for Hector (some believe just for the money.) The two were married in 1833, but the marriage only lasted a few years.

The music itself is a story of love and courting…and then a strange opium trip. The opening movement has visions of a splendid ball and a scene from a meadow. In the middle two movements take a strange turn into a strange and violent fantasy. The 4th movement is a drug-induced nightmare where he believes he has murdered his beloved (Harriet) and he is punished to death by a bloodthirsty crowd and is forced to watch his own execution. The 5th movement is set in hell at the "Witch's Sabbath," where demons and sorcerers, and even his Beloved, are celebrating his death.

You have already heard this music if you are a fan of movies. The movie *The Shining* has several excerpts of *Symphonie Fantastique*. The 5th movement *Dies Irae* can be heard several times throughout the movie. The main character's fall into insanity matches the themes of the music.

Breaking the Habit

Another song that could fall into the category of drug use as well as suicide, Linkin Park brought us *Breaking the Habit* in 2003. The song is the internal monologue of someone struggling with a drug habit and ultimately deciding to end their life. The singer is haunted by unresolved trauma in the past and finds temporary relief in the drug abuse. He tries to hide the addiction from others but decides to end the struggle. The song hits on topics of the internal struggle of someone with a drug addiction, self-doubt, isolation, self-harm, and shame.

The song was originally released on the band's second album *Meteora*. The sad ending to this song is that it is no longer performed by the band. In 2017, singer Chester Bennington took his own life. Singer Mike Shinoda says it is just too difficult to perform after Chester left. In 2017, Linkin Park debuted a new song at the tribute show to Chester Bennington, after he took his own life. The song is called *Looking for an Answer*. The lyrics were written by fellow vocalist Mike Shinoda.

Hashish

Sergei Lyapunov is not a well-known composer, but he had some impressive teachers. He was a pupil of Pyotr Ilyich Tchaikovsky and Sergei Taneyev. Composed around 1910, Lyapunov gave us the drug-induced *Hashish, an Oriental Symphonic Poem.* While his contemporaries were writing songs about wars and revolutions, Lyapunov gave us a musical poem that evokes scenes from a Middle Eastern harem. The music depicts the girls of the harem …. doing what they do while under the influence of hashish. The music flows between dreams and reality. The song pays homage to the Middle East, an area that was not well known at the time.

Hurt

"*It's not my song anymore*," said Trent Reznor, commenting on the success of someone else releasing his song. The song he wrote for the band Nine Inch Nails in 1994 on their *Downward Spiral* album. The song talks about self-harm and drug addiction. Some describe the song as a suicide note, while others describe it as flickers of hope during bouts of depression.

However it is described, the song *Hurt* became far more popular when country legend Johnny Cash covered it on his *American Recordings* album in 2002, just 9 months before his own death. In particular, the music video showed an intimate and vulnerable side of Cash that many fans connected with. Reznor praised Cash for his interpretation, in its "sincerity and meaning". A few other bands have tried to cover the song, at least during live performances, Mumford and Sons, and Sevendust, but none have done it justice like the Man in Black.

Drug and alcohol abuse seems to run rampant with heavy metal artists. There are so many more examples that could be added.

- Alice in Chains - Sick Man
  - written from the perspective of a man in the clutches of depression and drug abuse
- Saint Vitus – Dying Inside
  - Alcohol abuse
- Black Sabbath – Hand of Doom
  - A cautionary tale about American soldiers returning from Vietnam and turning to heroin.
- Ministry – Just One Fix
  - Heroin
- Guns N' Roses – Mister Brownstone
  - The band's slow fall into heroin
- Motorhead – Dead Men Tell No Tales
  - Heroin
- Tool – Sober
  - Written about a friend whose artistic side would only come out when they were high

12-Step Suite - Dream Theater

Written as a process across multiple albums, Dream Theater's Mike Portnoy originally conceived the idea of the 12-Step Suite as he was going through drug rehab, trying to kick his own alcohol and drug abuse. The 12 steps refer to the steps used in the Alcoholics Anonymous program. The song is also referred to as the AA Saga.

The pieces of the suite are individual songs written across five different Dream Theater albums. All lyrics were written by Mike Portnoy and are dedicated to Bill Willson, the founder of AA. Mike took his last drink in the year 2000.

The Glass Prison - Six Degrees of Inner Turbulence (2002)

I. Reflection
II. Restoration
III. Revelation

This Dying Soul - Train of Thought (2003)

IV. Reflections of Reality
V. Release

The Root of All Evil - Octavarium (2005)

VI. Ready
VII. Remove

Systematic Chaos - Train of Thought (2007)

VIII. Regret
IX. Restoration

The Shattered Fortress - Black Clouds and Silver Linings (2009)

X. Restraint
XI. Receive
XII. Responsible

The original plan was for Dream Theater to perform the entire suite after the *Black Clouds and Silver Linings* tour, but this also became the same time that Portnoy left the band. The suite was played as an entire work of music for the first time in 2016 for Portnoy's 50th birthday celebration concert while Mike was on tour with the members from the Neil Morse band and the band Haken.

When asked about the suite and his sobriety in a Loudersound interview, Portnoy stated," People *like myself who have chosen sobriety as a way of life, it doesn't mean we're going to drop out of society. We live in a society where there's drugs and alcohol everywhere. I have no problem with people that want to drink and do drugs – if they can do it in moderation, then God bless them. I wish I could, but I can't.*"

Abuse

A touchy subject that few artists ever try to take on is domestic abuse. Whether it is physical, verbal, or mental, trying to write about a subject that is so personal can be difficult. There are quite a few examples of abuse written into several operas, but difficult to narrow down as they are usually not featured.

- The Ring - Richard Wagner
    - Sieglinde - abused and forced into marriage by her hideous husband
    - Gutruna - psychologically abused by her half-brother and brother
- Norma - Vincenzo Bellini
    - Being cheated on

Rock and metal music is no different. Stories of abuse can be found across the various sub-genres.

- Janies Got a Gun - Aerosmith
    - Janie takes revenge on her father after years of sexual abuse
- Alice Cooper - Only Women Bleed
    - A ballad about a woman in an abusive marriage. Originally, many people believed the song was written about menstruation.

- Dont Let Daddy Kiss Me - Motorhead
    - Childhood sexual abuse
- Better Man - Pearl Jam
    - A woman trying to find the courage to leave her husband
- Rush - Everyday Glory
    - A child hiding while her parents' fight

It would be remiss to not include a couple of other songs from another genre. Both of these songs received severe backlash from critics but received praise from fans because they tried to tackle the subject of abuse.

- The Thunder Rolls - Garth Brooks
    - A woman waiting at home for her husband to arrive, knowing he has been with his mistress. In the live-concert-only 4th verse, she gets her revenge.
- Goodbye Earl - Dixie Chicks
    - Two longtime friends, Wanda and MaryAnne plot the murder of Wanda's abusive husband

Mental Illness

We have already seen one example of a story of mental illness earlier in this book - *Operation Mindcrime* by Queensryche. General mental illness has plagued musicians throughout time. Maybe there is a link between someone's mental health and the ability to write a powerful song.

In a 2009 study for Clinical Medicine, authors Marco Mula and Michael R. Trimble list psychopathologies of 22 famous composers that include major depressive disorders, bipolar disorder, psychosis, panic disorder, and alcoholism. Based on the issues we have seen in the previous sections, musicians are certainly prone to talk about their life experiences of drug abuse, alcoholism, depression, suicidal thoughts, and so many other personal things. The amount of practice time it takes to become a really good musician is incredible. Most of that time is spent alone. Going over the same passages again and again. For the classically trained musician, the practice room can be a lonely place. Hours and hours a day alone in a small room can certainly lead to many conditions including loneliness and depression.

Does it take a certain level of mental illness to write a really good song or any other really good artistic endeavor?

Six Degrees of Inner Turbulence

Dream Theater brought us a concept album that directly faces many types of mental illness. The 2002 concept album touches on subjects of alcoholism, loss of faith, self-isolation, and the sanctity of life and death. The title track, which is on the 2nd disc, is 42 minutes long (yes…that long! It's the whole second disc). The epic story is broken into 8 sections focused on 6 individuals and their different mental conditions: bipolar and post-traumatic stress disorder, schizophrenia, post-partum depression, autism and dissociative personality disorder.

Photo Credit - dreamtheater.net

Tracklist

Disc 1

1. The Glass Prison
2. Blind Faith
3. Misunderstood
4. The Great Debate
5. Disappear

Disc 2 - Six Degrees of Inner Turbulence

1. Overture
2. About to Crash
3. War Inside My Head
4. The Test That Stumped Them All
5. Goodnight Kiss
6. Solitary Shell
7. About to Crash (Reprise)
8. Losing Time/Grand Finale

Grief

There are plenty of songs that deal with the topic of grief and loss across all genres of music. Taylor Swift might have built a good portion of her career based on break-up songs. The break-up song becomes cannon fodder for the songwriter. But grief over a friend or loved one dying can also be a cathartic release for a songwriter to put emotions onto paper.

Previously we saw the band Mastodon write an album that was partially written as a tribute to the drummer's sister. But the band has been through so much more than just that one event. Grief has shaped their entire career. "*It feels like someone has to die for us to make an album*" - said guitarist Brent Hinds.

- *Crack the Skye* (2009) album was about Brann's sister who passed away at 14 years old.
- *The Hunter* (2011) album was a tribute to guitarist Brent Hinds' brother Brad, who passed away on a hunting trip.
- *Once More 'Round the Sun* (2014) was written in the wake of Brann's mother having fallen into a coma.

- *Emperor Of Sand* (2017) chronicles the cancer suffered by bassist Troy Sanders' wife, and Bill's mother, who passed away during recording.
- In 2018, they had to say goodbye to the longtime manager who passed away from pancreatic cancer.
- *Hushed And Grim* (2021) is about grief and loss after COVID.

"Writing and recording this record was like grief counseling for me: I started out feeling horrific and came out feeling fantastic. Even if we wanted to write a happier record, we couldn't. Our band doesn't work that way. We can't just shovel all of the darkness aside and say that everything was great." - Bassist Troy Sanders

Funeral March

Fredric Chopin's *Sonata No. 2 in B-flat Minor*. A stunning and haunting work. You've heard the song in nearly every funeral scene in movies, cartoons, TV shows. It's everywhere. Usually only the first couple of stanzas are played. The iconic melody has been used to embellish morbid humor.

The original tune for the funeral march is modeled after a Rossini opera, *La Gazza Ladra*, which was also used as the theme song for Alfred Hitchock's TV show. It is not exactly known why Chopin wrote the march, but it is thought to come out of the oppression and revolution of the Polish. Chopin's first biographer heard "the pain and grief of an entire nation."

The march has been used during the funerals for several heads of state, including John F. Kennedy, and ironically, Russian leaders Brezhnev and Stalin, the ones who created the oppression in the first place. Perhaps most tragically, the first time the Sonata was played as a Funeral March was for Chopin himself.

Adagio for Strings

Samuel Barber's *Adagio for Strings* has become the unofficial mourning song for the United States. It was used at Franklin Delano Roosevelt's funeral and after John F Kennedy's assassination. It was also played during many concerts after the 9/11 tragedy. In a concert just four days after Sept 11th, conductor Leonard Slatkin was set to perform with the BBC Symphony Orchestra. He knew he could not play happy songs, so he played *Adagio for Strings*. "*I knew that when it was over,*" Slatkin says, "*I'm visibly crying. I just left the podium, and I went into my dressing room and collapsed.*"

The piece first arrived in the US in 1938 on an NBC radio broadcast conducted by Arturo Toscanini, who had already seen many European Jewish colleagues murdered. A song written about oppression is now connected and associated with many historical events of mourning and loss.

The Best of Times - Dream Theater

Written by percussionist Mike Portnoy to his father as he was dying of cancer. The song includes lyrics of memories between the two. *"Portnoy recalls listening to the radio with his father and hearing the old radio shows. He also remembers going to the record shop and talking on the phone when they could be together."* The original demo version that was on the *Wither EP*, features Mike on vocals, instead of James Labrie. Mike was able to play the song for his father while in the hospital, then again sadly, at his father, Howard's funeral.

Mama Said - Metallica

Written as a memory, or as a prodigal son returning, *Mama Said* was written by James Hetfield of Metallica. James lost his mother to cancer when he was 16 years old. The song is written from the perspective of a son returning home, wanting to ask his mother questions about life, but being unable to because she is gone. It is a song of regret as James was not able to spend as much time with his mother as he would have wanted. (*If my math is correct*) The song was written roughly 17 years after her death and appears on Metallica's 1996 *Load* album. The band has only performed the song live three times.

Music has always helped people through emotional times. Songwriters use the medium to release their emotions into written lyrics. Composers write their emotions into feelings on a page of music. Using music to express emotion might be the best muse. Classical and Heavy Metal artists have written songs about suicide, drug abuse, mental illness, or the loss of a loved one. The writing process can be cathartic for the artist as a release of emotion, but it also creates great music, and the listener can express their own strong emotions while experiencing the music.

Sources for this section

1. Chillingworth, Alec. "Metallica: The Story Behind Fade to Black." Louder Sound, 5 February 2020, https://www.loudersound.com/features/metallica-story-behind-fade-to-black. Accessed 16 March 2024.
2. Terich, Jeff. "Gloomy Sunday: The Hungarian Suicide Song." Treblezine, 25 May 2015, https://www.treblezine.com/gloomy-sunday-hungarian-suicide-song/. Accessed 16 March 2024.
3. Genius.com. Billie Holiday. "Gloomy Sunday Lyrics." https://genius.com/Billie-holiday-gloomy-sunday-lyrics. Accessed 16 March 2024.
4. discogs.com, Master of Puppets, Accessed 10/13/24,https://www.discogs.com/release/3897415-Metallica-Master-Of-Puppets
5. Retter, Emily, Metallica drummer Lars Ulrich talks drink, drugs and rock and roll ahead of Glastonbury, Mirror, Accessed, 10/13/24, sethttps://www.mirror.co.uk/3am/celebrity-news/metallica-drummer-lars-ulrich-talks-3780401
6. Katsenelson, Vitaliy. "Tchaikovsky's Suicide Note." My Favorite Classical, https://myfavoriteclassical.com/tchaikovskys-suicide-note. Accessed 16 March 2024.
7. Berman, Boris. Stravinsky, Igor. "Autobiography." In Autobiography, ed. Walter Nouvel, 119-120. New York: W.W. Norton & Company, 1962. Accessed 16 March 2024. https://www.jstor.org/stable/j.ctt1npc15.
8. Berman, Boris. "Prokofiev: Piano Sonata No. 2 in Dm, Op. 14." Fugue for Thought, 24 October 2016, https://fugueforthought.de/2016/10/24/prokofiev-piano-sonata-no-2-in-dm-op-14/. Accessed 16 March 2024.

9. Utah Symphony. "Prokofiev Piano Concerto No. 2." https://utahsymphony.org/explore/2022/12/prokofiev-piano-concerto-no-2/. Accessed 16 March 2024.
10. Loud TV. "The Deadnotes - Azazel [official video]." YouTube, uploaded by Loud TV, 14 June 2016, https://www.youtube.com/watch?v=bWMWWQtKgJs. Accessed 17 March 2024.
11. Blabbermouth, "DISTURBED's DAVID DRAIMAN On 'Immortalized': 'I Just Want People To Walk Away Feeling Powerful'." 28 July 2015, https://blabbermouth.net/news/disturbeds-david-draiman-on-immortalized-i-just-want-people-to-walk-away-feeling-powerful. Accessed 17 March 2024.
12. Faceculture. "DISTURBED David Draiman about being labeled nu-metal, not copying other artists and stepping up (3/5)." YouTube, uploaded by FaceCulture, 10 December 2010, https://www.youtube.com/watch?v=eLDeFPMdKcw. Accessed 17 March 2024.
13. Disturbed, "Fighter of the Month." https://www.disturbed1.com/fighterofthemonth. Accessed 17 March 2024.
14. Daly, Joe. "Master of Puppets: How Metallica Created a Thrash Metal Anthem That'd Influence Generations." Louder Sound, 22 December 2021, https://www.loudersound.com/features/master-of-puppets-how-metallica-created-a-thrash-metal-anthem-thatd-influence-generations. Accessed 17 March 2024.
15. Barilla, Chris, Carrie Underwood and Papa Roach Team Up for Powerful 'Leave a Light On' Duet in Support of Suicide Prevention, People Magazine, Accessed 10/10/24, https://people.com/carrie-underwood-papa-roach-team-up-for-powerful-leave-a-light-on-duet-supporting-suicide-prevention-8688982
16. Nashville Symphony. "Fun Facts about Symphonie Fantastique." Nashville Lifestyles,

https://nashvillelifestyles.com/nashville-calendar/things-to-do/fun-facts-about-symphonie-fantastique/. Accessed 17 March 2024.

17. The Classical Girl. "The Halloween-ness of Berlioz's Symphonie Fantastique." The Classical Girl, Accessed 24 Mar. 2024, https://www.theclassicalgirl.com/the-halloween-ness-of-berliozs-symphonie-fantastique/.
18. Muller, Robert T. "Breaking the Habit." Trauma & Mental Health Report, 20 July 2020, https://trauma.blog.yorku.ca/2020/07/breaking-the-habit/. Accessed 17 March 2024.
19. Lyapunov, Sergei. "Hashish, Op. 46." Smart and Soulful Music, 2 March 2016, https://smartandsoulfulmusic.wordpress.com/2016/03/02/a-musical-high-day-3-hashish-by-sergei-lyapunov/. Accessed 17 March 2024.
20. Saving Country Music. "20 Years Ago Today, Johnny Cash Films the Video for 'Hurt'." , https://www.savingcountrymusic.com/20-years-ago-today-johnny-cash-films-the-video-for-hurt/, Accessed 24 Mar. 2024
21. Marshall, Clay, "I have no problem with people that want to drink and do drugs", Loudersound.com, 08/08/23, Accessed 11/5/24, https://www.loudersound.com/features/mike-portnoy-alcoholic-12-step-suite

22. The Twelve Step Suite, Dream Theater Wiki, Accessed 11/5/24, https://dreamtheater.fandom.com/wiki/The_Twelve-Step_Suite

23. Genius, "Sickman Lyrics." https://genius.com/Alice-in-chains-sickman-lyrics. Accessed 18 March 2024.
24. Tanos, Lorenzo. "The Real Meaning Behind Black Sabbath's 'Hand of Doom'." Grunge.com, 15 June 2021, https://www.grunge.com/713956/the-real-meaning-behind-black-sabbaths-hand-of-doom/. Accessed 18 March 2024.

25. Wiederhorn, Jon. "7 Insane Stories About the Creation of Ministry's 'Psalm 69'." Revolver, 18 May 2017, https://www.revolvermag.com/artist-artist-lists-news/7-insane-stories-creation-ministry%E2%80%99s-psalm-69/23523. Accessed 18 March 2024.
26. Ultimate Classic Rock, "Guns N' Roses - Mr. Brownstone." https://ultimateclassicrock.com/guns-n-roses-mr-brownstone/. Accessed 5 March 2024
27. Mills, Matt. "Tool's Sober: The Story Behind the Song." Louder Sound, 26 September 2019, https://www.loudersound.com/features/tool-sober-story-behind-the-song. Accessed 18 March 2024.
28. Hamori, Kate. "Women's Trauma and Opera." Classical Music Indy, 18 June 2018, https://classicalmusicindy.org/womens-trauma-and-opera/. Accessed 18 March 2024.
29. Marke B. "The Ring Cycle as Therapy: Francesca Zambello's SF Opera Production." 48 Hills, 27 June 2018, https://48hills.org/2018/06/ring-cycle-francesca-zambello-sf-opera/. Accessed 18 March 2024.
30. Kinney, Alison. "Norma Not: Believing Women." The Paris Review, 20 October 2017, https://www.theparisreview.org/blog/2017/10/20/norma-not-lie-believing-women/. Accessed 18 March 2024.
31. Scott, Jason. "Goodbye Earl by Dixie Chicks: Behind the Song." American Songwriter, 6 September 2018, https://americansongwriter.com/dixie-chicks-goodbye-earl-behind-the-song/. Accessed 18 March 2024.
32. Wilson, Miranda. "Musicians and Mental Health: A Toxic Culture Takes Its Toll on Players' Well-Being." Strings Magazine, 10 October 2019, https://stringsmagazine.com/musicians-and-mental-health-a-toxic-culture-takes-its-toll-on-players-well-being/. Accessed 18 March 2024.

33. Mula M, Trimble MR. Music and madness: neuropsychiatric aspects of music. Clin Med (Lond). 2009 Feb;9(1):83-6. doi: 10.7861/clinmedicine.9-1-83. PMID: 19271611; PMCID: PMC5922646.
34. Dream Theater, "Six Degrees of Inner Turbulence." https://dreamtheater.net/discography/six-degrees-of-inner-turbulence/. Accessed 19 March 2024.
35. Law, Sam. "How Collective Grief Shaped Mastodon's Most Grandiose, Gut-Wrenching Album Ever." Kerrang!, 19 September 2017, https://www.kerrang.com/how-collective-grief-shaped-mastodons-most-grandiose-gut-wrenching-album-ever/. Accessed 19 March 2024.
36. Blair, Elizabeth. "Chopin's Iconic 'Funeral March'." NPR, 1 March 2010, https://www.npr.org/2010/03/01/124039949/chopins-iconic-funeral-march. Accessed 19 March 2024.
37. Tsioulcas, Anastasia. "Samuel Barber's 'Adagio for Strings,' Tiesto, William Orbit: An American Anthem." NPR, 13 February 2019, https://www.npr.org/2019/02/13/694388226/samuel-barber-adagio-for-strings-tiesto-william-orbit-american-anthem. Accessed 19 March 2024.
38. Hetfield, James. Facebook. Juicy Guitars channel. Posted 4/16/24, https://www.facebook.com/share/p/XXa4vp2gtHMjaU4o/?mibextid=oFDknk
39. Richardson, Jake. "Rock and Metal Songs About Real Tragedies." Loudwire, https://loudwire.com/rock-metal-songs-about-real-tragedies/. Accessed 2 May 2024,
40. Dream Theater Wiki, "The Best of Times.", https://dreamtheater.fandom.com/wiki/The_Best_of_Times. Accessed 17 May 2024
41. Metallica Wiki. "Mama Said (song).", https://metallica.fandom.com/wiki/Mama_Said_(song). Accessed 17 May 2024

11.
A Perfect Circle

On a much happier note than the last chapter, the music has come full circle. For centuries, classically trained musicians have been writing and performing music. As we moved into the modern era, particularly after World War II, modern musicians were playing classical pieces in a modern format. In the early 1970s, we saw the creation of Heavy Metal music. In the 1980s, a few metal musicians studied and played classical music and incorporated it into metal music. Right at the end of the century, we find heavy metal bands collaborating with modern symphonies to support their music. In recent years there has been a surge of classically trained musicians playing heavy metal music.

S&M (Symphony and Metallica)

Recorded April 21-22 in 1999, Metallica collaborated with the San Francisco Symphony to bring the world a concert unlike most people had seen before. The original idea was presented to Metallica by the (then) director of the SF Symphony, Michael Kamen. Kamen was already well known as a movie score composer, working on major movies that include Robin Hood: Prince of Thieves, Die Hard, and Highlander, just to name a few. He had previously worked with Metallica on the song *Nothing Else Matters* but approached the band about doing a full collaboration with a wide range of the band's songs. After about a year of discussion, writing, and collaboration the two bands performed on stage together in a spectacular night. They even wrote a new song for the occasion called "- Human" or *Minus Human.*

This collaborative concert was accepted and loved by Metallica fans. It became a large commercial success and earned a shared Grammy for the performance of *Call of Ktulu.*

Author's Note - I had already owned the S&M album when I bought some very large speakers from a co-worker in 2000. Once I had the speakers setup, I had to decide what music was going to be played first. Of course, it was going to be Metallica's S&M. I put the CD in, closed my very thin door, and jammed out to the entire double album. Clearly annoying my family through the door, but they didn't complain. I later purchased the video of the concert. What I didn't realize is that the concert was part of the regular SF Symphony concert series. Half of the concertgoers were regular San Francisco Symphony season ticket holders, who showed up in tuxedos and formal dresses expecting to listen to a regular symphony concert. Half the concertgoers were hardcore Metallica fans who showed up in black concert shirts expecting a metal show. I think both fans were happy they were there.

To mark the 20th anniversary of the original concert, Metallica decided to recreate the concert. This time, Metallica brought the symphony to their venue, a sold-out arena, in September 2019. Metallica invited the San Francisco Symphony on stage with them inside the new 20,000-seat Chase Arena. The stage was centered in the arena, with fans all around, unlike a standard stage with the audience on one side of the musicians. While this is a standard setup for Metallica, it certainly would have been strange for the classical performers. The combined band did perform some of the same songs they originally did in 1999 but again added more.

Two of the highlights of these concerts were *The Iron Foundry* and *Anesthesia. The Iron Foundry* was originally written by Alexander Mosolov in 1927. The piece was part of an unproduced ballet called *Steel*. Subtitled "*The Music of the Machines*," *The Iron Foundry* evokes sounds and images of an actual steel factory with the pounding of heavy equipment. The (now) director of the symphony wanted to try to take the literal "heavy metal" theme into the concert. Instead of the symphony backing up on Metallica songs, this piece became Metallica backing up the symphony. The director wrote electric guitar parts to complement the original piece of work.

The second highlight of S&M 2 was *Pulling Teeth (Anesthesia)*. The original song was a bass solo on Metallica's first album in 1982, *Kill 'Em All*. The solo was written by bass player Cliff Burton. Burton passed away in 1986 due to a bus accident with the band. For the 2019 concert, the solo was done on acoustic stand-up bass by SF Symphony member Scott Pingle, who is the principal bass player. Current Metallica bass player Robert Trujillo said he was happy to step aside for this performance as he saw it as a tribute to Cliff and a special moment for James, Lars, and Kirk. Pingle not only played the original solo but added many elements of classical music into the performance.

Metallica's original performance with the San Francisco Symphony opened the doors for many more hard rock and metal artists to think about their music in a different light. Since 1999, there have been many more collaborations between a heavy metal band and a symphony.

- Scorpions and the Berlin Philharmonic Orchestra - 2001
- Yngwie Malmsteen and the New Japan Philharmonic - 2002
- Cradle Of Filth and the Budapest Film Orchestra - 2003
- KISS and Melbourne Symphony - 2003
- Nightwish and the London Philharmonic - 2004
- Aerosmith with the Boston Pops - 2006
- Dream Theater with "The Octavarium Orchestra," conducted by Jamshied Sharifi - 2006
- Katatonia and The Orchestra of State Opera - Plovdiv - 2017
- Def Leppard plays with the Royal Philharmonic - 2023

There will be more in the future. Not only are metal bands with full symphonies, but bands are also becoming symphonies, sort of...

Trans-Siberian Orchestra

If you have heard Christmas music in the last 20 years, you've heard the Trans-Siberian Orchestra. Originally started as a side project in 1996 by Paul O'Niell, Robert Kinkel, and Savatage's Jon Olivia, the trio set out to "create a progressive rock band that would push the boundaries." O'Niell was well versed in many different types of music from classical to broadway to Motown. He had been a touring guitar player for *Jesus Christ: Superstar* and producer for rock group Savatage, among many other positions. With Savatage, they had tried some conceptual pieces like *In the Hall of the Mountain King*, originally a classical piece by Edvard Grieg.The trio got together to form a "rock opera" band. They didn't have a focus yet, but they knew they wanted to join styles of music like The Who, classical, with over-the-top light shows like Pink Floyd. Their first idea was to do a trilogy of Christmas Rock albums. *Christmas Eve and Other Stories* was the first installment, and it became an immediate success. The album was quickly certified Double Platinum. With more than 30 members in the band, it really is an "orchestra." Multiple singers, both male and female, lead voices. Multiple guitar players, multiple keyboards, percussionists, violin, etc. As they tour, they will usually hire local string players for the performances.

Photo Credit - trans-siberian.com

As full of a circle as we can make it, there are now classically trained musicians who are playing heavy songs. Not only individual songs but forming bands simply to play metal music on traditional classic instruments.

Apocalyptica

Author's Note - While wandering through a record store, back when they had those, I stumbled across a unique album. Four Cellos Plays Metallica. That's strange. I had to buy it!

"*We just loved Metallica and we wanted to play it with the instruments we were able to play, which just happened to be cellos.*" says founding band leader Eicca Toppinnen

Photo Credit - apocalyptica.com

Just five months after their initial release, Apocalyptica opened a concert for their heroes. Metallica. There were originally four members of the group, Eicca Toppinen, Max Lilja, Antero Manninen, and Paavo Lötjönen formed in 1993. The founding members are all well-versed musicians and students at the world-famous Sibelius Academy in Helsinki, Finland. Their original goal was simple: play their favorite heavy metal songs on their preferred instrument, cello. Once they finally released their first album *Plays Metallica by Four Cellos*, the rest went very quickly. Five months after the release of their first album, Apocalyptica was on tour opening for Metallica, exposing their cello-flavored heavy metal to the hundreds of thousands of Metallica fans around the world.

Since 1996, Apocalyptica has released 10 studio albums. The 10th album was released in June of 2024 (*as this book was being written*) and is a return to the original concept, *Plays Metallica Vol. 2*. All the songs on this album will again be covers of Metallica songs, including spoken word vocals by James Hetfield and bass parts by Robert Trujillo of Metallica on various tracks.

The number of collaborations across albums two through nine with heavy metal artists is long and impressive; Dave Lombardo from Slayer, Corey Taylor from Slipknot, Cristinia Scabbia from Lacuna Coil, Adam Gontier from Saint Asonia, Nina Hagen, Tomoyasu Hotei, and Till Lindemann from Rammstein. The band has also been through several lineup changes. Sometimes, 3 members, sometimes 4, with Eicca and Paavo staying throughout. Apocalyptica has made an impact on the heavy metal world simply by sticking to the instruments they love, the cello.

Rodrigo and Gabriela

Rodrigo Sánchez and Gabriela Quintero originally started out as heavy metal guitar players, in and out of bands. In 1999, they decided to start a different journey and traded their electric guitars and heavy metal for acoustic guitars with Latino flair. They left Mexico and ended up in Dublin, Ireland as street performers.

In 2006, they put out their first album. Their influences were early rock and roll, heavy metal, country, pretty much everything. Their first big hits were covers of Led Zeppelin's *Stairway to Heaven* and Metallica's *Orion* off their self-titled debut album. Their music has also been featured on the TV show *Breaking Bad*, Monday Night Football (for Latino Heritage Night), and they even got to write and record with Hans Zimmer for *Pirates of the Caribbean: On Stranger Tides*.

In an NPR interview, Gabriela commented on the times they were busking in Ireland. "*We had to redefine what success meant. For us, it was traveling around the world and playing music*." I think she can redefine success again, in a more traditional sense.

Brass Against

While certainly not a classical group, *Brass Against* has turned some heads in recent years with their heavy metal covers done by a traditional jazz band. After Donald Trump took office in 2016, founder and guitarist Brad Hammond wanted an outlet as a form of protest to perform *Rage Against the Machine* songs. He formed a band and intended to do a one-night-only performance in 2018. The band is made up of standard jazz band instrumentation, saxophone, trumpets, trombone, percussion, piano, etc with guest vocalists to fill the voice parts on the cover songs. After the initial live performance, the band kept getting together to rehearse and started recording the performances and putting them on YouTube.

As of this writing, the YouTube channel has 257,000 subscribers and 70 videos with covers from Alice In Chains - Would?, Filter - Hey Man, Nice Shot, Led Zeppelin - Kashmir, Tool - 46 and 2, Deftones, My Own Summer, Danzig - Mother, Jane's Addiction - Mountain Song, Black Sabbath - War Pigs, Audioslave - Show Me How to Live, and the original Rage Against the Machine - Killing in the Name Of at 4.7 million views. Their version of Rage's *Wake Up* was featured in the 2021 film The Matrix Resurrections.

The YouTube channel became so popular and such a demand grew that Brass Against started touring. First, they started with single shows for festivals but then turned into full tours, taking along several singers to fill the vocals. The band Tool had Brass Against as their opening act during Tool's 2022 European tour.

There has been a circle of life created in the world of music between classical music and heavy metal music. Heavy metal artists teamed up with classical musicians and orchestras to support each other and play each other's music. After Metallica started it, many other metal bands have joined with various symphonies around the world to give the metal world a little different flavor to their music. Now there are classically trained musicians creating and playing heavy metal music. The two genres of music are blending more and more.

Sources for the section

1. Krovatin, Chris. "10 Times Rock and Metal Artists Collaborated with Classical Musicians." Kerrang!, https://www.kerrang.com/10-times-rock-and-metal-artists-collaborated-with-classical-musicians. Accessed 22 March 2024.
2. Ruskell, Nick. "Obey Your Maestro: Metallica, Cliff Burton, and Metal's Classical Heart." Kerrang!, https://www.kerrang.com/obey-your-maestro-metallica-cliff-burton-and-metals-classical-heart?next. Accessed 22 March 2024.
3. Pindiprolu, SK. "The Unforgettable Collaboration of Metallica, James Hetfield, and Lars Ulrich in S&M." Vocal Media, https://vocal.media/beat/the-unforgettable-collaboration-of-metallica-james-hetfield-and-lars-ulrich-in-s-and-m. Accessed 22 March 2024.
4. FamousComposers.net. "Michael Kamen.", https://www.famouscomposers.net/michael-kamen. Accessed 22 March 2024.
5. Morton, Luke. "Metallica's Robert Trujillo: 'S&M² Was One of the Most Powerful Experiences I've Ever Had'." Kerrang!, https://www.kerrang.com/metallicas-robert-trujillo-s-m2-was-one-of-the-most-powerful-experiences-ive-ever-had. Accessed 22 March 2024.
6. Los Angeles Philharmonic. "Iron Foundry, Op. 19." Hollywood Bowl, https://www.hollywoodbowl.com/musicdb/pieces/421/iron-foundry-op-19. Accessed 22 March 2024.
7. Trans-Siberian Orchestra. "About.", https://www.trans-siberian.com/about/origin. Accessed 23 March 2024.
8. Apocalyptica, "Biography." AllMusic, https://www.allmusic.com/artist/apocalyptica-mn0000594121#biography. Accessed 23 March 2024.

9. Apocalyptica Official Website, https://www.apocalyptica.com/. Accessed 17 May 2024
10. Hinojosa, Maria. "How I Made It: Rodrigo y Gabriela." NPR, 19 December 2019, https://www.npr.org/2019/12/19/789821334/how-i-made-it-rodrigo-y-gabriela. Accessed 23 March 2024.
11. Main, Nikki. "Who Are the Members of Brass Against?" The Sun, https://www.the-sun.com/entertainment/4065434/who-are-the-members-of-brass-against. Accessed 23 March 2024.
12. Lewry, Fraser. "Brass Against: Reinventing Protest Music in the Age of Trump and Brexit." Louder Sound, https://www.loudersound.com/features/brass-against-reinventing-protest-music-in-the-age-of-trump-and-brexit. Accessed 23 March 2024.
13. Kennelty, Greg. "Tool Announces Brass Against as Openers for European Tour." Metal Injection, https://metalinjection.net/tour-dates/tool-announces-brass-against-as-openers-for-european-tour. Accessed 23 March 2024.

12.
Conclusion

Heavy Metal music and Classical music are often seen as two separate musical entities. The groups of people that listen to the two styles are different, they dress differently, one group has less tattoos, etc. It is easy to spot a metal fan in the wild. Black concert shirt, usually long hair, black leather. There is a general "uniform" that headbangers wear. Not the same for the classical music fan or musician. The music is the combining element.

From Brian Posehn, the heavy metal stand-up comedian -

"I love metalheads, when I mention metal, people go crazy because you have to give it up. You never see a guy with this shirt off screaming "R&B!!" Metalheads are different from any other fan of music. We have our own symbol that means metal. You just do that to another metalhead and he's just like "Indeed."

Throughout this book, we have looked at various aspects of the overlapping of the two styles of music: heavy metal and classical. There are many aspects of the styles that are similar.

A good story to drive the lyrics or theme. Rush gave us a song about the future of mankind. Mozart gave us a story about a playboy who was sent to hell. Turandot is about trying to marry the princess. Dream Theater told us a tale about meeting a strange man, and Metallica played three songs to show us how someone can grow over time. So many songs have been written about the experience of going to war, losing battles, and winning wars. Even a good book can be the basis for great music. Several musicians have tackled J.R.R. Tolkien's tales. The concept album is not a new feature to music; Holtz gave us The Planets, and Volbeat gave us the Wild West. King Diamond gave us the plot of a horror movie with Abigail. A good story can be the backdrop of so many good songs and albums.

Changing the sound or instrumentation to bring more volume out or even creating new instruments to get the sound you want. The guys from Marshall brought forth the Marshall stack and changed the volume of rock and roll forever. Richard Wagner not only added more musicians to increase the volume but also created his own instruments to get the sound he wanted. It wasn't just Wagner that gave us different instruments. There are a variety of metal bands that have used non-traditional instruments to change the color of their music.

Using unique musical tones and intervals to evoke feelings of uneasiness and discomfort. The Devil's Tone was discovered long ago and was banned for a while by the church. Black Sabbath revived the tone and turned it into an entire style of music that would later be named Heavy Metal. They just wanted to make music like horror movies.

Using odd and non-traditional time signatures to give the listener a different musical experience. While most songs are written in common time because it is easy, many artists delve into the odd signatures to change the feel of the music. Dream Theater gave us possibly the hardest song with the most time changes. The band Tool uses time signatures in collaboration with the themes to move the music in different ways. Stravinsky was known for bending the rules of music and not only played with time signatures but also with taboo themes.

Not only using religion as a topic but also getting people to think about their own religious experience. There are several stories that have crossed paths with the same theme; someone sells their soul to be a great musician. Did they actually make a deal with the devil, or did they just practice until their fingers bled? Bach would write music for the church as a job to follow in his father's footsteps, but it was a means to make money. Dante wrote a whole tale about the levels of hell. The Devil can be a great source of musical literature if you want to push the norm and get people to think.

The Virtuoso is a term used for someone that is particularly skilled in the field of music. While these people are admired and celebrated, what most people don't see is the years of hard work and dedication to the craft of music. The long hours of learning. There have been many virtuosos across the years. For classical music the preferred instruments were piano (or harpsichord), or violin. In modern music, it is the guitar or drums. Mozart and Van Halen should be used in the same sentence when talking about high-level musicians.

Diving into taboo subjects to share experiences, act as a personal release, or express an artist's own journey into the harder sides of life. Suicide, drug use, Abuse, Mental Illness, and grief have all been subjects the artists have written about. Sometimes they write to share a warning tale. Sometimes they write to tell the world about their experience. Sometimes they write to release their own emotions. Whatever the purpose, creating music that focuses on topics that bring people down can be hard to listen to, but audiences will react positively as they share in the experience.

There are more connections between Heavy Metal music and Classical music than there are differences. While the fans may look different, the music connects the fan bases. Even the fans of one style are playing the music of the other.

What now?

Now that you are coming to the end of this book, maybe you want to explore more.

Not sure where to go from here? Let me help you!

Are you a metalhead who would like to explore more about classical music? (Is this starting to sound like a Choose Your Own Adventure book?) I would make two suggestions.

First - Start with something you know, specifically, movies. As mentioned early in this book, movies are the modern version of operas. The soundtracks to movies are the modern-day version of what Mozart used to write. But instead of just watching the movies, focus on the music, particularly big epic movies. The bigger the budget, the bigger the name of the composer they can afford. John Williams, of course, is probably the biggest name in modern movie soundtracks. Indians Jones, Schindler's List, Jurassic Park, Saving Private Ryan, Harry Potter, and of course Star Wars. Next time you watch one of these movies, close your eyes and listen to the music. What music is playing? Who is on screen? What is happening in the scene? You'll start to notice some similarities.

Take Star Wars, for example. Everyone knows the Star Wars theme. It's the song that plays during the scrolling yellow text. You can almost think of that song as the Star Wars Overture. Within that song, you'll get to hear some of the bits from the other songs that are coming later. You hear some big sections, and some quiet sections. The big song sets up the rest of the music for the movie. Then pay attention to the other sections of music. Each main character is given their own theme. Vader's March. Everyone knows that, even my daughter. It's written low and slow. Big drums. Very pompous. Which key is it written in? What's the tempo? Vader's theme gets reprised in Episode Six, as Luke is trying to help an injured Vader off the Death Star. You can hear a very soft Theme getting played in the background. It's still Vader's theme, but is it the same notes? Is it the same tempo?

In contrast is Luke's Theme. It's the one where Luke is standing outside at dusk, staring at the double sun, with the long notes played by the French horns. It's very ethereal. Very much in contrast to Vader's Theme. Who else in the movie series gets their own theme song? I would take this same idea and listen to some other big movies like Harry Potter or Lord of the Rings. Does the main song introduce themes in the music? Do different characters get their own song?

Secondly - My other suggestion as a metalhead is to start with some hard-hitting classical music. Many of the songs I listed in this book would fall under this category but let me give you some more ideas. When I was a kid, I remember a commercial for the Time-Life collection called Classical Thunder. My mom actually bought it, and I would listen to all of these songs, many of which were already mentioned in this book, like the 1812 Overture. Here is a list to look into.

1. Also Sprach Zarathustra - Also known as the theme from 2001: A Space Odyssey.
2. Romeo and Juliet, Suite No. 2 - Prokofiev – Yes, it's a song written about that play you probably DIDN'T read in high school. But it's a good song.
3. Sabre Dance - Gayane - Really quick song, think Speed Metal, but for strings.
4. In the Hall of the Mountain King - Peer Gynt - This one does start off slow and quiet, but don't let that fool you. It finishes in a whirlwind of speed.
5. Les Toreadors - Carmen Suite No. 1 - Bizet - I would love to hear this song played on electric guitar.
6. Tchaikovsky - Piano Concerto No. 1 - One of the heaviest piano songs that I love, at least the beginning.

I hope these suggestions will point you in a direction to enjoying different aspects of music.

But are you on the other side - Are you a classical musician that wants to learn more about heavy metal music? I also have some suggestions for you. Like classical music, heavy metal is broken into different categories. Some metal heads would say that you must like it all. No, you don't. There are several sub-genres of metal I personally stay away from. Just not my thing. Some metalheads only listen to one genre and ignore everything else. Some dabble in a little of everything. I'm not going to list them all…this book doesn't need to be that long. Here are a few of the sub-genres of Heavy Metal and a description of each.

- Progressive Metal - Probably the most talked about category in this book. This is often a category where the style of the band doesn't fit any other subgenre, so they are put here. Rush, Dream Theater, Mastodon, and Tool are some of the big names. Often full of very accomplished and talented musicians, these players are highly skilled, and songs can take on multiple styles of music. Often very long, epic pieces of music.
- Thrash Metal - This style brought the Big 4 - Metallica, Megadeth, Anthrax, and Slayer, along with other bands like Testament, Kreator, and Suicidal Tendacies. These bands are known for their blazing-fast speed in guitar playing.
- Power Metal - This combines some speed from Thrash Metal and symphonic context with fantasy-themed songs. Iron Maiden, Judas Priest, Dio, and Scorpions are some of the big names.
- Death Metal - This is one of the extreme subgenres using heavy distortion and low-tuned guitars. The lyrical subjects are often occultist, morbid, and dark. Venom, Possessed, and Morbid Angel are a few of the bands in the category.
- Black Metal - Yes, there is a slight difference between Death and Black Metal. While the guitars will sound similar, the singer in Black Metal is often singing in a higher range. The facepaint is more prevalent in bands like Mercyful Fate, Bathory, and Celtic Frost.
- Symphonic Metal - This is a combination of Progressive, Thrash, and orchestral music. Often, these bands will incorporate an actual orchestra or at least have keyboards playing those parts. This is also where you are likely to find a classically trained female lead singer, singing in soprano, high above the heavy bass riffs. Nightwish, Lorna Shore, Epica,

Lacuna Coil, and even Trans-Siberian Orchestra would fall into this category.

- Viking Metal - Yep! That's a thing. If you would like a history lesson about Viking culture in your music, this one's for you. Full of slow, heavy riffs and rhythmic choruses. Amon Amarth, Hammerheart, and Einherjer all use Norse mythology and lore as music subjects.
- Hair Metal - That stuff from the 1980s. Full of hairspray and spandex. Also known as Glam Metal. The songs are full of pop-influence, simple guitar riffs, and slow power ballads (must get the girls somehow). Those who survived the debauchery of the 80s managed to put out a few decent albums. Van Halen, Motley Crue, Poison, and Skid Row were some of the biggest names.
- Nu Metal - A term many of the bands don't like, this genre was formed in the late 1990s to early 2000s. This style combines some elements of thrash and alternative, then mixes them with elements of hip-hop to give us a unique mix of music. In a diverse style of bands, we get Korn, Limp Bizkit, Slipknot, Disturbed, and Linkin Park.
- Neo-Classical Metal - Heavily associated with individual players, more than whole bands. Yngwie Malmsteen is considered the one who started the genre, but others like Tony McAlpine, Vinne Moore (UFO), Paul Gilbert (Racer X), and Marty Friedman (Megadeth) have filled in the style in later years. These are all highly trained guitarists who play more in a Baroque style rather than traditional Speed or Thrash style.
- And there are at least 20 other genres and subgenres of Metal music. Feel free to explore.

That was a bunch of information. Let's see if I can make this less complex…

Do you like…	Listen to…
Big full sounds in your music	Power Metal, Neo-Classical Metal OR Wagner and Tchaikovsky
A high soprano voice	Symphonic Metal, Progressive Metal OR Various Operas
Many fast notes	Thrash Metal, Progressive Metal, Neo-Classical OR Paganini or Les Toreadors
Epic, moving storylines	Progressive Metal, Power Metal, Viking Metal OR, Operas or Holst

It is my hope that whichever side of this book you started on, Classical or Metal, you learned something about the other side.

I'm sure someone is going to say, "You forgot about this or that song." Yeah, I probably did. I could have just kept adding examples and made the book much longer. I hope I have enough examples that you will want to explore on your own. Maybe you found a song you liked and want to listen to more. Maybe you will appreciate that song more the next time you hear it. It is my hope that other styles of music are not as scary as you thought. Thank you for reading.

www.ingramcontent.com/pod-product-compliance
Ingram Content Group UK Ltd.
Pitfield, Milton Keynes, MK11 3LW, UK
UKHW062312290726
14090UKWH00018B/1031